decorative
wirework

decorative
wirework

a contemporary approach to a traditional craft

consultant editor: **simona hill**

southwater

This edition is published by Southwater

Southwater is an imprint of Anness Publishing Ltd
Hermes House, 88–89 Blackfriars Road
London SE1 8HA
tel. 020 7401 2077; fax 020 7633 9499
www.southwaterbooks.com; info@anness.com

© Anness Publishing Ltd 2004

UK agent: The Manning Partnership Ltd
6 The Old Dairy, Melcombe Road, Bath BA2 3LR
tel. 01225 478444; fax 01225 478440
sales@manning-partnership.co.uk

UK distributor: Grantham Book Services Ltd
Isaac Newton Way, Alma Park Industrial Estate
Grantham, Lincs NG31 9SD
tel. 01476 541080; fax 01476 541061
orders@gbs.tbs-ltd.co.uk

North American agent/distributor
National Book Network, 4501 Forbes Boulevard
Suite 200, Lanham, MD 20706
tel. 301 459 3366; fax 301 429 5746
www.nbnbooks.com

Australian agent/distributor: Pan Macmillan Australia
Level 18, St Martins Tower, 31 Market St, Sydney, NSW 2000
tel. 1300 135 113; fax 1300 135 103
customer.service@macmillan.com.au

New Zealand agent/distributor: David Bateman Ltd
30 Tarndale Grove, Off Bush Road, Albany, Auckland
tel. (09) 415 7664; fax (09) 415 8892

A CIP catalogue record for this book is available from the
British Library.

Publisher: Joanna Lorenz
Editorial Manager: Helen Sudell
Editor: Simona Hill
Designer: Nigel Partridge

Previously published as part of a larger volume,
Decorative Tin & Wirework

10 9 8 7 6 5 4 3 2 1

The publisher would like to thank the
following people for designing projects
in this book:

Lisa Brown for the Beaded Wire
Candlesticks p50–51.

Diane Civil for the Swirled Candle
Sconce p70–72.

Andrew Gilmore for the Festive Light
Bush p32–33, Toasting Fork p42–43,
Flower Fly Swatter p82, Heart-shaped
Trivet p83, Toilet Tissue Holder p84–85,
Bottle Carrier p86–87, Egg Tree p89–91,
Hanging String Dispenser p96–97,
Spoon Rack p102–103, Garden Drinks
Carrier p114–115.

Dawn Giullas for the Pocket Clips p27
and Greetings Cards p28.

Karin Hossack for the Window Box
Edging p24–25, Mesh Place Mat p39–39,
Pretty Plate Edging p40–41, Woven Pipe
Cleaner Basket p92–93 and Decorative
Shelves p100–101.

Alison Jenkins for the Panelled Flower
Pot Cover p22–23, Desk Accessories

p34–35, Picture Frame p44–45 and
Fabric-covered Baskets p94–95.

Mary Maguire for the Happy Hippy
Necklace p26, Angel Decoration
p29–31, Decorative Candle Sconce
p46–47, Filigree Chandelier p55–57,
Bicycle Toy p73–75, Wire Vegetable
Basket p98–99, Toast Rack p104–105,
Copper Bowl p110–111, Wire Bird
Feeder p124, Garden Lantern p112–113,
Spice Rack p116–117, Garden Tray
p118–119, Utility Rack p122–123.

Sue Radcliffe for the Flower Lampshade
p60–61, Jewel Nightlight p64–65.
Classic Candlesticks p68–69 and
Monogrammed Clothes Hanger p80–81.

Jennie Russell for the Spiral Napkin
Holders p36–37, Flower Holder p58–59,
Fiesta Oil Bottle p66–67.

Adele Tipler for the Woven Bottle
p48–49, Fused Flowers p62–63 and
Woven Chair p107–109.

Stewart Walton for the Bent Wire
Chandelier p52–53, Rolling Pin Holder
p88, Kitchen Hook Rack p120–121.

Contents

Introduction

Light, malleable and attractive, wire lends itself to being manipulated and sculpted into decorative and useful objects for the home and garden. Wire is available in a range of sizes and can be twisted, wrapped, coiled or woven to form light, airy decorative objects or more solid, sturdy structures. Wire is usually rustproof

so it is particularly useful for creating objects for the kitchen and bathroom where steam and damp conditions would soon mar a less resilient material. Different types of wire – soft aluminium wire, green plastic-coated gardening wire, beautiful copper wire, even coloured pipe cleaners – can be used to produce a variety of textures, shapes and designs. A wire coat hanger can be opened up and reshaped into something even more useful, and sheets of chicken wire can be

moulded and transformed into fantastic sculptures.

In this book you will find all the information you need to start making both beautiful and useful objects for your home. Beginning with a description of the different types of wire that can be used, the

first chapter goes on to describe the tools you will need and provides a clear guide to the skills and techniques you will learn. Once you have mastered the basics, you can start making some of the step-by-step projects. Each project has a symbol that indicates the level of skill required. The symbol ⚥ indicates that it is suitable for a complete beginner. The projects with ⚥⚥⚥⚥⚥ indicate that an advanced level of skill and knowledge is required.

Decorative Wire Objects shows you how you can create intricately worked items for your home, from fabulous candlesticks and sconces, beaded napkin holders and delicate place mats to original greetings cards and jewellery.

Practical Wire Objects concentrates on more essential, although no less decorative, items. The projects use a range of simple skills and techniques to

produce useful and practical objects, including an attractive lacy-effect vegetable basket, a handy string dispenser, an elegant egg tree, a flower-shaped fly swatter, and a variety of inspirational storage ideas for all sorts of household items. More challenging projects include a stylish coiled toast rack, and weaving wire to make a striking chair seat and a unique and colourful bird feeder.

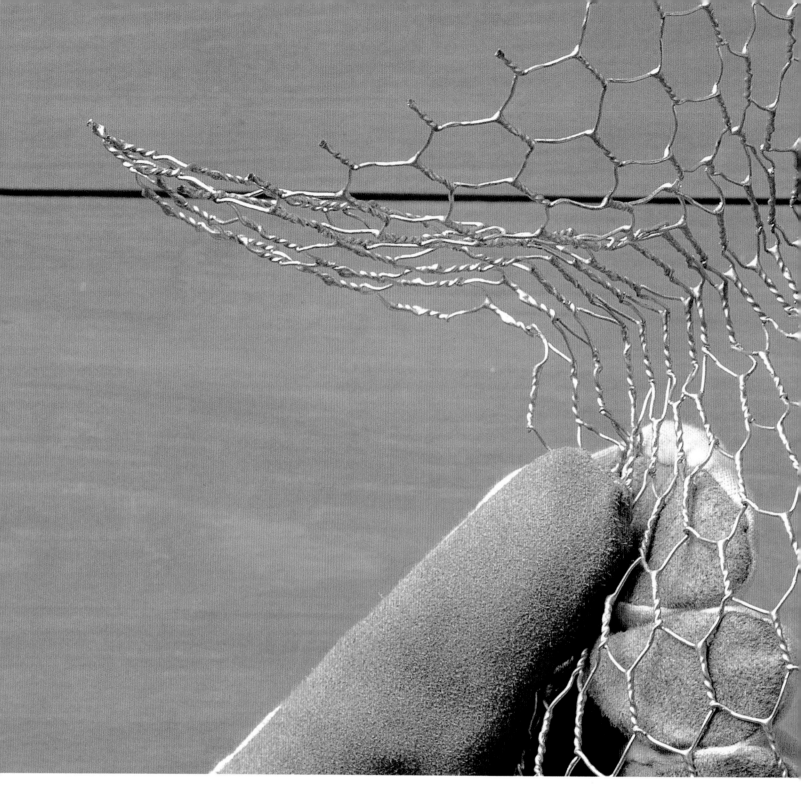

Wirework

Basics

Before beginning any craft project, it is important to have an understanding of the essential materials and equipment, and the basic skills and techniques. In wirework, these include using different tools to twist, wrap, coil and weave a variety of wires, and sculpting and moulding chicken wire safely. Once you have mastered the basics, you will be able to attempt any of the projects in this book, and even create some of your own.

You can buy wire from good jewellery, craft and sculpture suppliers, as well as some hardware stores. There are also specialist wire suppliers, and electrical stores may also stock the materials you need.

Materials

Aluminium wire

This is a dull blue-grey colour. It is the easiest to work with because it is so soft and easy to bend.

Chicken wire

This is made from galvanized steel wire. Usually used for fencing and for animal pens, it comes with different-sized holes and in a range of widths. The projects in the book call for the smallest gauge. Chicken wire is easy to manipulate and inexpensive.

Copper wire

This has a warm colour and comes in different tempers (hardnesses). Soft copper wire is easy to work with and is available in a broad range of gauges.

Enamelled copper wire

Used in the electronics industry, this is available in a wide range of colours.

Galvanized wire

This is zinc-coated steel wire. The zinc coating prevents rusting, making it ideal for outdoor use. Galvanized wire is hard, so does not bend easily. This wire is springy, so needs to be used with caution. Available in five gauges.

Garden wire

This is easy to manipulate as it is plastic-coated. It is perfect for kitchen or bathroom accessories because it is waterproof, long-lasting and colourful.

Pipe cleaners and paper clips (fasteners)

These less obvious wirework materials are great fun to work with.

Silver-plated copper wire

This wire is particularly well suited to jewellery making and fine wirework.

Straining wire

This strong, textured wire is made of strands of galvanized wire twisted together. Take care when using it.

Tinned copper wire

This is shiny and does not tarnish, so it is suitable for kitchenware.

Twisty wire tape

This thin, flat tape with a wire core comes in green for gardening and blue and white for household use.

Wire coat hangers

These are cheap and widely available.

The most important tools for wirework are a good pair of wire cutters and some pliers. General-purpose pliers will be sufficient for some projects, although round-nosed pliers are a worthwhile investment.

Equipment

Parallel (channel-type) pliers – These are suitable for straightening bent wire and for bending angles.

Round-nosed pliers – Also known as snug-nosed jewellery pliers, these can be used for many different crafts, as well as for repairing broken jewellery. Use to bend wire into tiny circles.

Rolling pin, wooden spoon, pencil, broom handle

Many household objects are useful to coil wire around.

Ruler or tape measure

Many projects require very accurate measurements to ensure a good result.

Scissors

Use to cut through thin wire.

Wire cutters

Choose cutters with good leverage and long handles.

Gardening gloves and goggles

These protect your skin when working with scratchy wire. Wear goggles when manipulating long lengths of wire, especially if the wire you are using is under tension.

Hammer

A hammer is useful for flattening the ends of cut lengths of wire.

Hand drills

Useful for twisting soft wires together.

Permanent marker pens

Use to mark measurements on wire.

Pliers

General-purpose pliers – These often have serrated jaws to give a strong grip. Place a piece of leather between the pliers and the wire to prevent any marking.

Needle-nosed pliers – These are very useful for reaching into difficult places and are the best pliers for working with chicken wire.

Wooden coat hangers

These can be used to twist galvanized wire together. Make sure the handle is secure and will not unscrew.

Wooden form

To bend strong wire into small circles use a wooden mould. Drill a screw into a piece of wood, but leave the head protruding from the wood. Bend the wire around the screw.

These instructions will help you with the basic wirework techniques used to make the projects in this book. Try to familiarize yourself with this section before embarking on any of the projects.

Techniques

Twisting Wire

This is a simple and effective way of joining two or more wires to add strength and texture to a design. Soft wires, such as copper, are easiest to twist, and using a hand drill speeds up the process. The harder wires, such as galvanized wire, require more effort. If you use a coat hanger to twist wires, choose the wooden type with a wire hook that revolves, ensuring that the handle is securely attached and will not unscrew.

Twisting Hard Wire

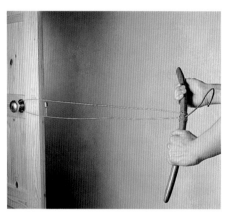

1 Cut a piece of wire three times as long as the required twisted length. Double the length of wire and loop it around a door handle or other secure point. Wrap the loose ends on one side of the coat hanger hook. Make sure you hold the wire horizontally, otherwise you may get an uneven twist.

▶ **3** To release the tension in the wire, hold the hanger firmly in one hand and grip its hook in the other. Quickly release your hold on the hanger, which will spin around a bit. Remove the wire from the handle and cut off the ends.

2 Keeping the wire taut, begin turning the coat hanger. Do not relax your grip as this may cause an uneven texture. Twist the wire to the degree required, taking care not to overtwist as the wire may snap.

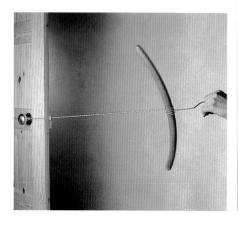

Twisting Soft Wire

1 Double the lengths of wire to be twisted, by folding it in the middle. Two lengths have been used here, and you can use wires with different finishes. Loop the wires around a door handle and wrap the other ends with masking tape before securing them into the hand-drill chuck.

2 Keeping the wire taut, rotate the drill to twist the wire to the degree required. Start slowly at first so that you can gauge the tension. With soft wires there is no need to release the tension in the wire before removing them from the drill bit and trimming the ends.

Wrapping Wire

When wrapping wire, ideally the core wire should be both thicker and harder than the wrapping wire. Copper wire is the most suitable to use to wrap around a core. When cutting the core wire, remember to allow an excess length of at least 6.5cm/2½in to form a winding loop. The long lengths of soft wire used in wrapping can be unmanageable, so coil the wire first, as described in method B.

Method A

1 Using round-nosed (snug-nosed) pliers, make a loop at the end of the core wire. Neatly attach the wrapping wire to this loop.

2 Insert a pencil or other suitable object into the loop and use it as a winder. While winding, hold your thumb and index finger right up against the coil to ensure that the wire is closely wrapped.

Method B

1 Using round-nosed (snug-nosed) pliers, make a loop at the end of the core wire and bend the wire into the desired shape along half its length. Form a loop at the other end of the core wire and secure the wrapping wire to the loop. Insert a pencil into the loop and use it as a winder.

2 Wrap part of the wire, remove the pencil and coil the wire that has been wrapped. Now use this section as the winder. Use your hand to support the core wire from beneath, with the wrapping wire running between your fingers and thumb.

Tips for Wrapping Wire

When using wire from a skein, keep it on the floor with your foot holding it in place. This will help you achieve the necessary tension for wrapping the wire and prevent the wire skein from unravelling and knotting.

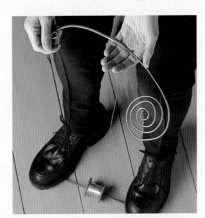

When using wire from a spool, it is easier if you insert a long stick through it and hold it in place with your feet. This will allow the spool to unwind quite freely while keeping the wire sufficiently taut.

Making Coils Coils are probably the most commonly used decorative device in wirework. They also have a practical use as they neaten and make safe what would otherwise be sharp ends. The flattened extended coil is a common structural and decorative device used in wirework. It is a quick and easy way to make the side walls of a container, for instance.

Open Coils

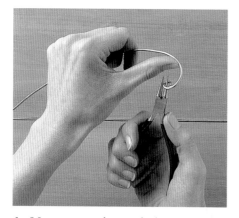

1 Using round-nosed (snug-nosed) pliers, make a small loop at the end of the wire. Hold the loop in the pliers, place your thumb against the wire and draw the wire across it to form a curve. Use your thumb to supply the tension.

2 Use your eye to judge the space left between the rings of the coil. If the wire is thicker, you will need more tension to make the curve and it will be more difficult to make the curve evenly spaced.

3 Finally, carefully flatten the coil with parallel (channel-type) pliers. Bend the coil into shape carefully.

Closed Coils

1 Using round-nosed (snug-nosed) pliers, make a small loop at the end of the wire.

2 Hold the loop securely with parallel (channel-type) pliers. Bend the wire around the loop until you have a coil of the size required. Keep adjusting the position of the pliers as you work.

Right: Ornate and stylish, wirework coils are surprisingly simple to make.

Flattened Extended Coils

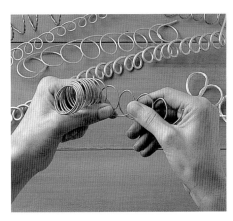

1 Wrap the wire several times around a broomstick or other cylindrical object to give you a coil. If using galvanized wire, you need to brace your thumb firmly against it.

2 After removing the coil from the broomstick, splay out the loops one by one, holding them firmly between your fingers and thumbs.

3 Keep splaying out the loops until the whole coil has been flattened. The loops will now look more oval than round. You can stretch the coil further to open the loops if you wish.

Weaving Many basketwork and textile techniques can be applied to wirework. Knitting and lacemaking techniques can also be employed with great success. Fine enamelled copper wire is especially suitable for weaving as it is soft and pliable and comes in a wide range of colours. Of the techniques described here, methods B and C will give a more closely woven and tidier finish than method A. Method A is the simplest.

Method A

The quickest and easiest way to weave is to wind the wire in and out of the struts to create an open texture.

Method B

Pass the wire under each strut before looping it around the strut to create ridges in the weave.

Method C

Weave around the struts by passing the wire over each strut and looping it around the wire to create a smooth, closely woven surface. This result is similar to method B but the rib will be on the outside.

Chicken Wire Techniques

Chicken wire is malleable and light, making it ideal for creating large structures. For ease of explanation, the instructions refer to struts (the horizontal, twisted wires in the hexagons) and strands (the single wires). Wear gloves when you work. Finish off any project by tucking away all the sharp ends.

Binding Wire – Method A

Place a length of wire along the edge of the chicken wire. Using a thinner wire, bind the length of wire and the chicken wire together.

Binding Wire – Method B

When binding diagonally, bind along the diagonal strands of the chicken wire. Bind evenly, taking in each strut as you come to it.

Transforming Hole Shapes

Hexagonal hole shapes give chicken wire lots of moulding potential and the shapes are easy to make.

Hearts

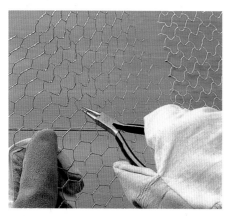

Hold the centre of each strut in turn with round-nosed (snug-nosed) pliers and twist up the wire to each side to create a cleft in the centre. When this process is repeated a pattern of heart shapes will emerge.

Brick Wall

Insert pliers into the holes in the wire so that the sides of the pliers are up against the struts. Pull the handles gently apart to transform each into a rectangle shape. Work carefully to keep the mesh from buckling.

Fishing Net

Hold the wire secure with small pliers and then pull it with general-purpose pliers to elongate the holes. You could hook the chicken wire over some nails hammered into a piece of wood if you were stretching a larger area.

Joining Chicken Wire

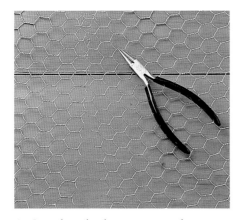

1 Cut the chicken wire at the point just before the wire strands twist into struts so that one of the edges is a row of projecting double strands and the other is a row of projecting struts.

2 Place the projecting struts on top of the other piece so that they overlap slightly. Using round-nosed (snug-nosed) pliers, carefully wrap each of the projecting strands around the corresponding strand on the upper-most piece of chicken wire.

3 Twist the overlapping struts firmly together using round-nosed pliers.

Shaping Chicken Wire

Chicken wire can be shaped into any number of shapes. For extra strength, work with the struts running horizontally and for a more elegant shape, work with the struts running vertically.

Shaping with Vertical Struts

Shaping with Horizontal Struts

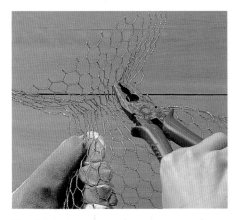

1 Using general-purpose pliers, squeeze the struts together to form the neck, pulling all the time to elongate the wires. To make the bulge, stretch out the holes by inserting general-purpose pliers as described for the brick wall effect, but only stretch them a little for a more elegant shape.

2 Using round-nosed (snug-nosed) pliers, squeeze the struts together to make the bottom tip, pulling again to elongate the wires.

Make the hexagons heart-shaped. Squash the cleft in each heart with round-nosed pliers. Mould with your thumbs. To make the bulge, mould with your fingers from inside, pulling out with pliers. To make the bottom tip, squash the clefts, contracting them to form a tight core.

Decorative
Wire Objects

Wire is available in a variety of thicknesses and strengths and can be used in a multitude of ways to create imaginative and decorative items for the home. You can make fabulous jewellery, charming ornaments, unusual greetings cards and picture frames, elegant candle sconces and candlesticks, and even mesh tablemats, to name just a few. Be bold and explore the decorative potential of wire.

Twist and Sculpt

Once you have mastered the skill of using pliers, working with wire is easy, though labour intensive, and the results can be quite spectacular.

There are many types of wire, in a variety of thicknesses and colours. All wires, however, possess the same quality of malleability, enabling you to bend, coil, shape and sculpt them. Pipe cleaners come in a whole range of vivid colours, and are easy to use – you don't even need pliers – making them ideal wires for children to experiment with. Another wire that is commonly used in wirework is galvanized wire.

This doesn't rust, so it's a good material to use to make projects for the garden. Other lightweight wires used in these projects include enamelled copper wire and aluminium wire. You can also use coat hangers, which are

good for sculpting unusual shapes, and even wires from inside telephone cabling.

The instinctive thing to do with wire is to bend it into decorative motifs. Stars, flowers, hearts and circles are a few easy shapes you could try. Once you

feel proficient try small-scale sculptures, perhaps using gold, or silver-plated wire for hanging ornaments, or motifs for a greetings card. In addition to bending wire, you can also twist two different types of wire together to create unusual

textures and subtle colours. Twisted or plaited (braided) wire can be used decoratively. Alternatively, coiling wire around a cylindrical object such as a broom handle or pen, gives spirals of wire, which can be used as edging, as springs or to provide delicate decoration. Amazingly, lightweight wire can be knitted to create a mesh-like effect, or woven to make a basket.

Wire is often used as a framework in a project, to which more elaborate wire decorations are added. For larger and more complicated projects, you can create separate parts of an item, and then solder the units together. For extra sparkle, glass beads can be threaded on to wire coils, or you can also spray-paint galvanized wire with metallic paints to inject more colour into the finished piece.

Fan-shaped panels of opaque polypropylene are the perfect foil for the light, silvery wire framework around this pot. The wire stitching used to attach the plastic to the framework makes an interesting feature.

Panelled Flower Pot Cover

you will need

flower pot base, circumference 33cm/13in, height 15cm/6in

paper

soft pencil

ruler

scissors

polypropylene sheet

long-nosed pliers

galvanized wire, 2mm/$\frac{1}{13}$in, 1mm/$\frac{1}{25}$in and 3mm/$\frac{1}{8}$in thick

wire cutters

cutting mat

bradawl (awl)

soldering iron, solder and flux

1 Using the template provided at the back of the book, make a pattern to fit around the outside of your flower pot. If your pot is not the specified size, adjust the template to fit by scaling it up or down on a photocopier.

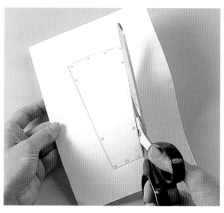

2 Make another paper template that shows just one of the opaque panels of the pot cover. Mark on this the stitching holes for the panels. Cut around the edge of the shape carefully.

3 Using a soft pencil, trace around the second template on to the sheet of polypropylene. Cut out four pieces. Use different colours, if you like.

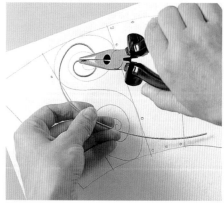

4 Using pliers, curl a piece of 2mm/ $\frac{1}{13}$in wire to match the S-shape design. Repeat to make four matching S-shapes.

5 Working on a cutting mat and using a bradawl (awl), pierce small holes around the edges of the plastic panels where indicated on the template.

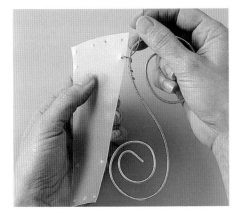

6 Using 1mm/¹⁄₂₅in wire, neatly bind the S-shapes to the plastic sections. Join all four of the plastic sections together in this way with a wire shape between each one. Trim any untidy wire ends.

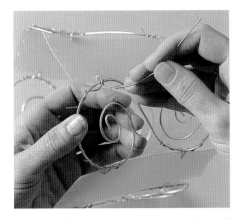

7 Bind the last wire shape and panel together to complete the pot shape. Bend any panels that have become mis-shaped back into shape.

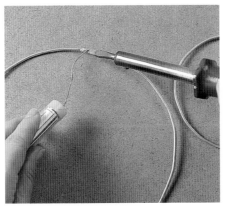

8 Cut two lengths of 3mm/¹⁄₈in wire to fit around the top and the base of the pot cover. Solder the ends of each length together.

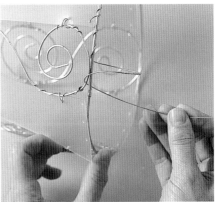

9 Bind the top and bottom rings to the pot cover using the 1mm/¹⁄₂₅in galvanized wire. Trim the ends neatly. Place the flower pot in the cover.

Galvanized wire is ideal for the garden, as it will not rust when exposed to the elements. Use this pretty repeating heart to edge a window box, or even to add an orderly edging to an unruly garden border.

Window Box Edging

1 Scale up the template at the back of the book to a height of 15cm/6in, as a guide for bending the wire. Cut a 43cm/17in length of galvanized wire and bend it in half. Hold the centre point with pliers and twist the two ends around each other twice.

2 The loop forms the centre of the heart. Bend the two tail ends around the loop to form a small heart shape, using the scaled-up template as a guide. Cross the wires at the bottom of the heart. Try to make the heart shape symmetrical.

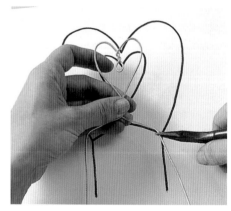

3 Hold the heart with pliers just above the crossing point and twist the two free ends around three times.

4 Use the pliers to bend the two free ends out and down, following the template.

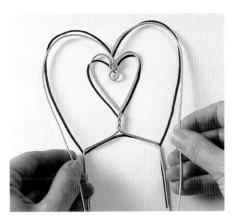

5 Cut a 48cm/19in length of wire, bend it in half as before and loop the central point over the twisted loop in the small heart. Use pliers to flatten the loop, then bend the wires down following the template.

6 Align the wire ends from the small and large hearts on each side, and twist them tightly together. Use wire cutters to even up the wire at the bottom of the twists. Ensure the ends are long enough to add stability.

These necklaces are great fun to create and are the perfect project to make with children. You could also make matching accessories using clip-on earring backs and headband bases.

Happy Hippy Necklace

you will need
round-nosed (snug-nosed) pliers
plain, furry and thick, bumpy
pipe cleaners
coloured paper clips (fasteners)
twisty wire tape
wire cutters

1 Using round-nosed (snug-nosed) pliers, make small flowers from plain pipe cleaners. Make the flower centres by straightening paper clips (fasteners) and coiling them into spirals. Bend a furry pipe cleaner into a five-petalled flower. Twist the ends together.

2 Coil a plain pipe cleaner and striped paper clip into tight, neat spirals to make the centre of the largest flower. Cut a length of twisty wire tape and tie a knot in it. Thread it neatly through the flower centre so that the knot sits at the front.

3 Bend a thick, bumpy pipe cleaner to form the necklace. Bind the small flowers to the pipe cleaner necklace with the twisty tape, tucking in the tape ends behind the flowers. Bind the large flower to a paper clip and clip on to the pipe cleaner necklace.

4 Form a loop at each end of the pipe cleaner and attach twisty wire tape to each loop. Form two paper clips into cones, then slide them on to the ends. Bend the ends of straightened paper clips into coils. Join them together to make two chains. Attach the chains to the ends of the pipe cleaner. Make a "hook-and-eye" from paper clips.

Adorn your pockets with these highly original and decorative clips. Galvanized wire has been used here; this can be sprayed with metallic car paint to change its colour.

Pocket Clips

you will need

wire cutters

galvanized wire, 1mm/$^1/_{25}$in and

0.6mm/$^1/_{41}$in thick

ruler or tape measure

round-nosed (snug-nosed) pliers

half-round pliers

1 Cut a 1m/40in length of 1mm/$^1/_{25}$in galvanized wire. Make a coil at one end with the round-nosed (snug-nosed) pliers. Bend the wire to make an S-shape, referring to the diagram above. Square off the loop below the coil with half-round pliers.

2 Using half-round pliers, nip in the wire to form one side of the neck, then make a large loop in the wire. From top to bottom the large loop measures 11.5cm/4½in. Make a mirror-image loop and coil on the other side of the large loop, cutting off any excess wire.

3 Fold the structure in half and bend the top of the large loop at both sides to make shoulders. Nip in the bottom of the large loop to make a scallop. Using the 0.6mm/$^1/_{41}$in wire, bind the coils together. Bind the neck for 12mm/½in.

A homemade card makes a personal gift that will be cherished. The instructions here show you how to make the cherub Valentine card, but templates are also provided for the other ideas.

Greetings Cards

you will need

33 x 21.5cm/13 x 8$\frac{1}{2}$in red cardboard

21 x 14.5cm/8$\frac{1}{4}$ x 5$\frac{3}{4}$in pink cardboard

paper and felt-tipped pen

scissors

ruler

gold spray paint

round-nosed (snug-nosed) pliers

galvanized wire, 0.6mm/$\frac{1}{41}$ in and 1mm/$\frac{1}{25}$in thick

wire cutters

straight pin

needle and thin nylon thread

masking tape

red cotton thread

paper glue

1 Fold the red cardboard in half. Make the heart templates. Centre the small heart on the red cardboard, 2.5cm/1in from the bottom. Centre the large heart on the pink cardboard, 1.5cm/$\frac{3}{5}$in from the bottom. Cut out the hearts, reserving the pink. Spray the pink cardboard bottom gold.

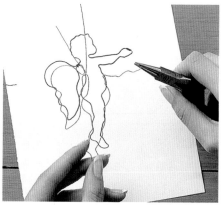

2 Use the round-nosed (snug-nosed) pliers to bend the thinner wire all around the template of the cherub. Make two. Bind the top of the wings. Form two hearts from the thicker wire. Using a pin, mark the position of the cherubs and one heart, with pairs of holes on the pink cardboard.

3 Attach the cherubs and heart to the pink cardboard by stitching through the holes with the nylon thread. Secure the ends with masking tape. Hang the second wire heart from the first heart with cotton thread. Centre the pink cardboard on the red and glue in place. Glue the pink heart inside.

Once you have become dextrous at sculpting in wire, try making this elegant Christmas angel that is sure to take pride of place hanging on the Christmas tree. The soft silver-plated copper wire is easy to bend.

Angel Decoration

you will need

silver-plated wire, 1mm/$\frac{1}{25}$in thick

round-nosed (snug-nosed) pliers

parallel (channel-type) pliers

wire cutters

narrow ribbon

star-shaped bead or crystal droplet

1 Photocopy the template at the back of the book, enlarging it to the size you require. Leaving 5cm/2in at the end, bend the wire around the angel template, using round-nosed (snug-nosed) pliers and your fingers.

2 Make the hair and the forehead up to the eye. Make the lower lid of the eye, then the upper lid. Halfway along the upper lid, make a loop to form the pupil. Squeeze the corner of the eye with parallel (channel-type) pliers.

3 Shape the nose and make a larger loop around the end of the round-nosed pliers for the nostril. Shape the mouth, closing the lips with parallel pliers, then shape the chin. Refer to the template as you work.

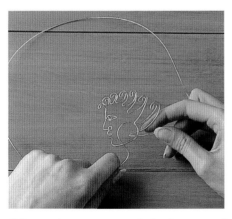

4 Loop the wire around the bottom of the hair to make the cheek. This loop will help to keep the structure flat and more manageable.

5 Follow the template along the arm. Make loops with round-nosed pliers for the fingers, and shape the bottom line of the arm.

6 Make the outline of the shoulder by carefully looping the wire around the point where the top of the arm joins the neck. ▶

7 At the waist, bend the wire across to form the waistband. Make a series of long horizontal loops with slightly curled ends back along the waistband to represent floaty fabric. When you have made seven loops, secure with a tight twist at the bend.

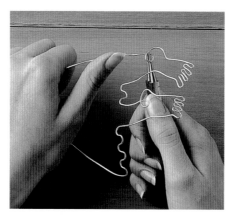

8 Make a large curve for the lower part of the skirt. Shape a wavy hem around the thickest part of the round-nosed pliers. The legs interrupt the hemline. Make the toes in the same way as the fingers, but make them shorter and rounder. Shape the heels and make a loop at each ankle.

9 Continue bending the wire to complete the wavy hemline and make another, shorter curve to form the back of the skirt. Secure the lower section of the angel by twisting the wire around the waistband as tightly and neatly as possible.

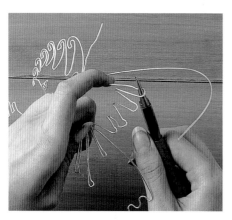

10 Make overlapping loops along the bottom of the wing. Form the curved top of the wing.

11 Loop the wire around the back of the shoulder and also under the bottom of the wing. Finish off with a coil and cut off the wire.

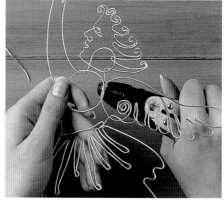

12 Using the 5cm/2in of wire left at the start, bind the shoulder and wing together. Cut off the end. Thread the ribbon through the waistband loops and then hang a star-shaped bead or crystal droplet from the angel's hand.

This pretty floral decoration will make a sparkling centrepiece on your Christmas table, but it would also create a magical effect as temporary garden lighting for a party on a summer evening.

Festive Light Bush

you will need

wire cutters

dark green plastic-coated garden wire,
2mm/$\frac{1}{13}$in and 1mm/$\frac{1}{25}$in

ruler or tape measure

flower-shaped fairy (decorative)
lights, 12v

pliers

broom handle

large pebble

artificial leaves with wire stems

flower pot

sand

1 Cut a length of the thicker garden wire to the same length as the fairy (decorative) light flex (electric cord) and then turn a neat loop in one end with pliers.

2 Carefully bind the fairy light flex to the thicker garden wire using the finer garden wire. End the binding at a point 20cm/8in beyond the last fairy light.

3 Make coils in the length of bound wire by winding it around a broom handle, as shown.

4 At the end of the bound section, wrap the free end of the thick wire around a large pebble.

5 Arrange the coiled wire in a bush shape. Support the coils by wiring them together, if necessary.

6 Attach the artificial leaves to the coiled wire at regular intervals by winding their stems around it.

7 Half-fill a flower pot with dry sand. Put in the pebble, then support the plant stem with more sand.

8 Adjust the fairy lights so that they are completely clear of the wires and the leaves.

Organize your desk with this smart wire stationery set. The pen pot and note holder are modern wire sculptures, and the notebook has a matching motif. Complete the set with designer paper clips.

Desk Accessories

you will need

paper

pencil

galvanized wire, 2mm/¹⁄₁₃in, 3mm/¹⁄₈in and 1mm/¹⁄₂₅in thick

wire cutters

long-nosed pliers

ruler or tape measure

soldering iron, solder and flux

florist's wire

scissors

thick cardboard

hardback notebook

craft knife

cutting mat

bradawl (awl)

coloured paper

PVA (white) glue

1 Enlarge the spiral, triangle and flower templates from the back of the book to the required size. Cut lengths of the 2mm/¹⁄₁₃in galvanized wire with wire cutters and then use long-nosed pliers to bend the lengths of wire so that they match the spiral, triangle and flower designs. Set the wire shapes aside.

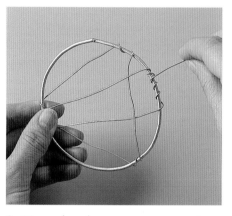

2 To make the pen pot, cut three 30cm/12in lengths of the 3mm/¹⁄₈in galvanized wire and bend them into circles. Use a soldering iron to join the ends. Stretch some lengths of florist's wire across the centre of one of the rings to form the foundations for the base of the pen pot. Wrap the ends of the florist's wire around the ring to secure.

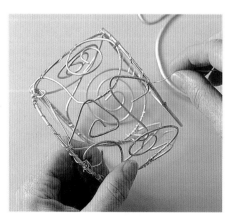

3 Using 1mm/¹⁄₂₅in wire, bind several shapes to the base and to each other to form the sides. Bind on another ring and repeat. Add the third ring to make the top and cut out and insert a circle of thick cardboard in the bottom.

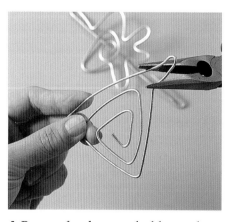

4 Repeat for the note holder, making two squares for the top and base. To make a paper clip, cut a 35cm/14in length of 3mm/¹⁄₈in wire and bend one end to match one of the template shapes.

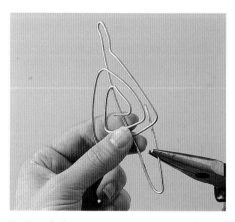

5 Bend the remaining wire so that it runs down behind the centre of the shape and extends below it, as shown. Take the end and bend it back on itself to form a large paper clip (fastener).

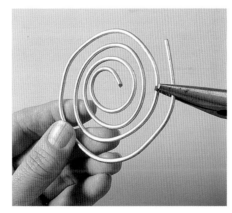

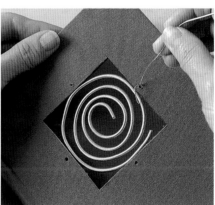

6 For the notebook, use a craft knife to cut a square from the front cover of a hardback notebook. Pierce a small hole halfway along each side of the window using a bradawl (awl).

7 Bend a length of 3mm/⅛in wire into a spiral shape to fit the window in the book cover.

8 Stick a sheet of coloured paper to the inside of the cover. Place the spiral inside the window then bind it to the book using florist's wire.

Simple copper coils with a random sprinkling of brightly coloured glass beads make attractive napkin rings. If you are designing a buffet table setting, scale up the design to make a paper napkin holder.

Spiral Napkin Holders

you will need

wire cutters

ruler or tape measure

copper wire, 0.8mm/$\frac{1}{31}$in and 1.5mm/$\frac{1}{19}$in thick

pen or wooden spoon

assorted glass beads

long flat-nosed pliers

cardboard tube from a roll of foil or clear film (plastic wrap)

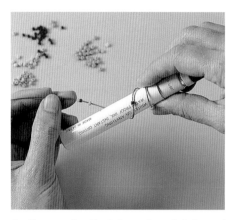

1 Cut a 1m/1yd length of 0.8mm/$\frac{1}{31}$in copper wire and wind it on to a pen or the handle of a wooden spoon. As you form each loop, add a few small glass beads in assorted colours.

2 Form 18 coils to make a tight spring, then slide it off the pen or wooden spoon. Twist the two ends of the wire tightly together using long flat-nosed pliers.

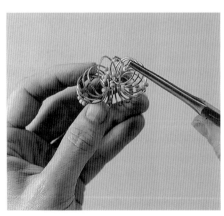

3 Add a small bead and pull the ends of the wire around it to secure.

4 To make a larger ring, use 1.5mm/$\frac{1}{19}$in copper wire and larger beads. Form the coils around a cardboard tube, such as the inside of a roll of foil or clear film (plastic wrap).

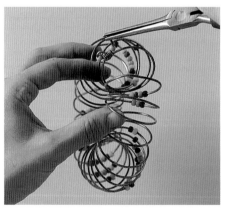

5 Make a small tight coil of 0.8mm/$\frac{1}{31}$in copper wire using long flat-nosed pliers and slide it over both ends of the ring. Pull the small coil tight. Add a bead to each end of the large ring and loop the ends of the wire over the bead to secure it.

Although it looks intricate, there is nothing more to this colourful tablemat than plain knitting and a simple double crochet stitch. Crystal seed beads add to the glittering effect.

Mesh Place Mat

you will need

50g/2oz each of enamelled copper wire in burgundy and pink, 0.4mm/$\frac{1}{63}$in thick

pair of knitting needles, 2.75mm/ size 12/US 2

ruler or tape measure

crochet hook, 2mm/size 14/B-1

wire cutters

crystal seed beads

sewing needle

1 Using the burgundy enamelled copper wire and knitting needles, loosely cast on 52 stitches. Knit every row with an even tension until the work measures 22cm/8½in. Use another combination of colours for the wire if you prefer.

2 When you reach this length, pull the work from the sides and from the top and bottom to stretch the mat out to the final measurement of 23 × 29cm/9 × 11½in. If necessary, add a few more rows to correct the length, then cast off loosely.

3 Using pink wire and a crochet hook, loosely chain crochet 165 stitches. Turn the work, miss one chain, then double crochet/single crochet into every chain. At the end of this length cut the copper wire, leaving a 2.5cm/ 1in tail.

4 Thread 82 crystal seed beads on to a length of pink wire. Holding several seed beads in your left hand, work along the edging strip again in double crochet, adding in one seed bead to every other double crochet stitch.

5 Work another two rows in double crochet and cast off. Measure the finished edging around the mat and stretch evenly if necessary to make it fit. Thread a sewing needle with pink wire. Starting in a corner of the mat, stitch on the pink edging.

Turn the plainest plate into something special, using flattened wire coils. Bind two layers of coils together with a simple overcast wrap of lilac enamelled wire, which adds a subtle touch of colour.

Pretty Plate Edging

you will need

aluminium wire, 2mm/¹⁄₁₃in thick

ruler or tape measure

wire cutters

30cm/12in length of dowel or stiff cardboard tube, 1cm/½in thick

white dinner plate, 26cm/10¼in in diameter

masking tape

flat-nosed pliers

pencil

terry towel or cloth

rolling pin

25g/1oz reel of lilac enamelled aluminium wire, 0.6mm/¹⁄₄₁in thick

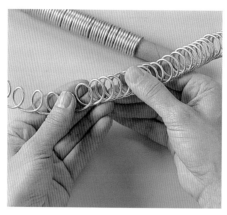

1 Measure and cut a 3m/10ft length of aluminium wire, and wrap it around a piece of 1cm/½in dowel. Spread the coil so the loops are approximately 5mm/¼in apart, and then flatten it. Working from one end, prise open the flattened rings, leaving a small gap between each.

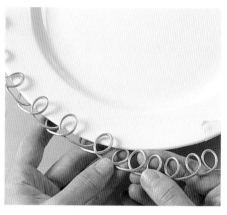

2 Bend the flattened coil into a circle, with the rings facing inwards towards the plate. Place it around the edge of the plate and press it firmly into position by pushing one ring under the rim and the next over the top. Use masking tape to hold the end in place as you work.

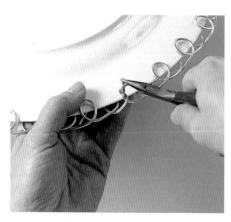

3 Push the last ring under the rim, then turn the plate over. Remove the tape and adjust the spacing of the first and last rings to match the rest. Open out the ends of the wire and twist them together using pliers. Press them towards the base of the plate.

4 Cut a 3.6m/12ft length of wire. Coil it around a pencil and spread the rings out so that there is a 3mm/⅛in gap between them. Place the coil on a terry towel or cloth and use a rolling pin to flatten it. Pull the coil apart so a gap shows between the rings.

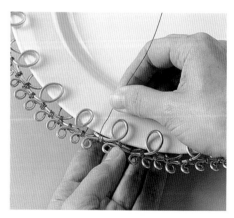

5 With the rings turned out, position the small coil around the outside edge of the large coil. Bind using the enamelled aluminium wire. Wrap the fine wire three times around each loop of the small coil and then fasten off securely.

Toasting English muffins over an open fire in winter is always a pleasant activity. This toasting fork is made from four coat hangers and is both light and strong.

Toasting Fork

you will need

4 wire coat hangers, straightened

wire cutters

ruler or tape measure

wooden spoon

tacking wire

permanent marker pen

galvanized wire, 0.8mm/¹⁄₃₁in thick

general-purpose pliers

piece of copper piping

hammer

1 To make an inner strut, measure 10cm/4in from the end of one of the straightened coat hangers and wind it around a wooden spoon at this point to create a loop. Measure 2cm/¾in before bending the remaining length of wire straight.

2 Make a second strut a mirror image of the first by winding the wire the other way around the wooden spoon.

3 Make the two outer struts in the same way. This time allow 12.5cm/5in for the prongs and bend a right angle 2cm/¾in beyond the prong loop.

4 Bind the struts together temporarily with tacking wire, loosely enough to allow movement.

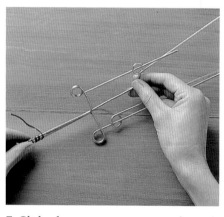

5 Slide the two outer prongs through the loops of the inner prongs. Measure up from the prongs and mark the handle at 4, 18, 4, 20, 4 and 2cm, or 1½, 7, 1½, 8, 1½ and ¾in intervals. Using galvanized wire, bind the 4cm/1½in sections. Do not trim the excess binding wire from the top section.

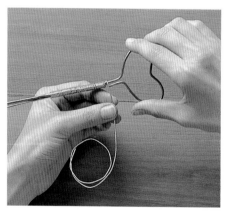

6 Cut off three of the remaining strut wires at the last mark. Form the fourth strut wire end into a heart shape, using pliers and bending it around a piece of copper piping to create the curves. Leave 2cm/¾in at the end. Bind it in with the other three wires, still using the binding wire.

7 Using the pliers, grip each wire in turn halfway along the 20cm/8in section. Pull the wire so that it bows out. This will be the fork handle so test it in your hand for comfort and adjust if necessary. Trim the ends of the prongs so that they are even and hammer each tip flat.

This imposing little picture frame is made from nothing more than cardboard, galvanized wire and metallic paint, yet it looks weighty and solid, and even has its own wire stand.

Picture Frame

you will need

paper and pencil

galvanized wire, 2mm/^{1}/$_{13}$in, 3mm/^{1}/$_8$in and 1mm/^{1}/$_{25}$in thick

wire cutters

ruler or tape measure

long-nosed and flat-nosed pliers

soldering iron, solder and flux

thick white cardboard

craft knife

steel ruler

cutting mat

double-sided adhesive tape

bradawl (awl)

silver metallic paint

paintbrush

epoxy resin adhesive

1 Trace the frame template from the back of the book and enlarge it as required. Use the wire cutters to cut four lengths of 2mm/^{1}/$_{13}$in wire each 70cm/28in long. Using the long-nosed pliers, bend each length of wire so that it matches the spiral and zigzag shapes along the outer edges of the frame.

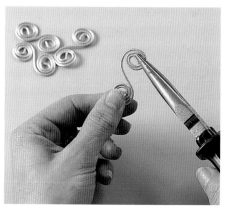

2 For the decoration, cut ten lengths of 2mm/^{1}/$_{13}$in wire each 30cm/12in and curl each one into a tight S-shape using long-nosed pliers. Cut a 40cm/16in length of 3mm/^{1}/$_8$in wire and bend into a square to form the centre of the picture frame, arranging the ends in the middle of one side. Solder the ends together.

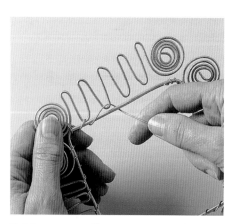

3 Using 1mm/^{1}/$_{25}$in wire, neatly bind the four decorative side sections to the central frame.

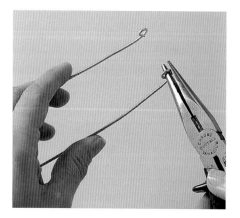

4 For the stand, bend a 30cm/12in length of 2mm/^{1}/$_{13}$in wire into a U-shape. Curl each end into a tight loop using flat-nosed pliers. Centre it on the back of frame at the top and bind in place with 1mm/^{1}/$_{25}$in wire.

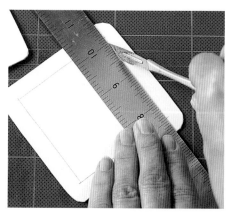

5 Cut two pieces of cardboard to fit the frame. Cut a window from the front and a slightly larger window from the back. Reserve the cut-out window from the back. Stick the frames together using double-sided tape.

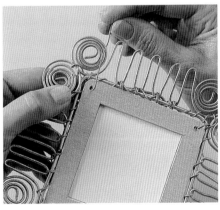

6 Using a bradawl (awl), pierce a small hole in each corner of the cardboard picture holder. Paint the front and edges silver.

7 Bind the picture holder to the frame at each corner using short lengths of 1mm/¹⁄₂₅in wire.

8 Use epoxy resin adhesive to glue the S-shapes to the front of the frame. Insert the picture and replace the reserved square to hold it in place.

Despite its ornateness, this medieval-looking candle sconce is quite easy to make. By making the base of the basket wider and weaving the sides deeper you can adapt the shape to fit a larger candle.

Decorative Candle Sconce

you will need

copper wire, 1.5mm/^{1}/19in and 0.8mm/^{1}/31in thick

ruler or tape measure

wire cutters

general-purpose pliers

masking tape

round-nosed (snug-nosed) pliers

parallel (channel-type) pliers

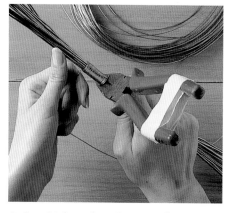

1 Cut 21 lengths of 1.5mm/^{1}/19in wire, each 38cm/15in long. Bundle together so that they are even at the top and bottom, and grip them with the general-purpose pliers 16cm/6¼in from one end. Hold the pliers closed with masking tape so they act as a vice. Using the 0.8mm/^{1}/31in wire, bind the bundle of wires for 2cm/¾in from the pliers. Do not cut off the wire. Release the pliers.

2 Using round-nosed (snug-nosed) pliers, bend a downward-curving loop at the end of each wire. Bend down the wires at right angles at the top of the bound section so they spread out in a circle. Using the 0.8mm/^{1}/31in wire that is still attached to the bundle, weave around the wires to make a base with a diameter that measures 7cm/2¾in. This will form the base of the basket.

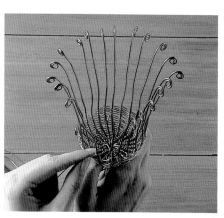

3 Bend up the wires at the edge of the circle and weave the side of the candle basket to a depth of about 2.5cm/1in.

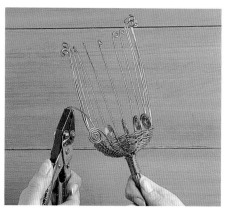

4 Using parallel (channel-type) pliers, coil down the wires to the edge of the candle basket.

5 Using parallel pliers, make two columns of coils with the wires left under the candle basket. Make nine coils in each column, ensuring that the second column is a mirror image of the first. Trim the end of each wire, increasing the amount you cut off by 12mm/½ in each time, so that the coils decrease in size. Using round-nosed pliers, form waves in the remaining wires. Trim the ends of the outer wires, so that the central one is the longest.

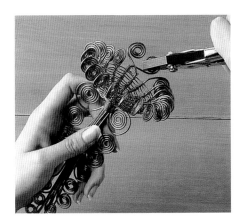

6 Decide which is the back of the sconce. Using the parallel pliers, unwind the two coils at the back a little, cross them over each other and twist flat. Attach the sconce to the wall through the holes in these two coils. Bend back the wavy wires so that they support the sconce at the bottom, holding it away from the wall. Check the distance between the candle flame and the wall.

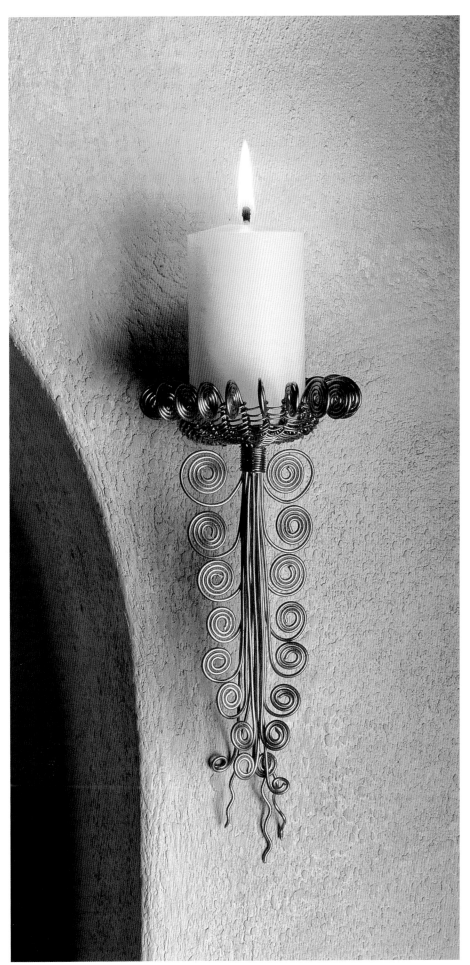

Here's an unusual way of recycling those beautiful bottles that are too nice to throw away. This technique requires patience, but it is not difficult to master.

Woven Bottle

you will need
bottle
enamelled copper wire in two colours,
1.5mm/¹⁄₁₉in and 0.6mm/¹⁄₄₁in thick
ruler or tape measure
wire cutters
masking tape
round-nosed (snug-nosed) pliers

1 Cut four pieces of 1.5mm/¹⁄₁₉in wire 25cm/10in longer than twice the height of the bottle. Cross the wires on the base of the bottle and bend them so that eight struts run up the sides of the bottle. Tuck the wire ends inside the neck and wrap tape around the body and neck of the bottle.

2 Join a doubled length of the 0.6mm/¹⁄₄₁in wire to the point where the wires cross and start weaving. For this project, pass the wire over each strut and then loop it around the strut before continuing to the next one. The rib will be covered by the weave at this stage.

3 Loop the wire around each strut, creating a smooth and closely woven surface. Change wire every so often to achieve a striped pattern. Continue around the sides of the bottle, twisting the wires where you join them.

4 When you have woven to the top of the bottle, pull out the ends of the wire struts from inside the bottle. Using the round-nosed (snug-nosed) pliers, make downward-curving coils.

5 Continue to weave the fine enamelled copper wire around the coils. You will now see the reverse pattern of the weave. Secure the last end of wire by wrapping it several times around a strut before cutting it off.

Twisted silver wire, sparingly threaded with beads, has a delicate yet sculptural quality. An assortment of decorative glass beads, following a colour theme, look wonderful entwining a pair of glass candlesticks.

Beaded Wire Candlesticks

you will need
ruler or tape measure
wire cutters
medium silver wire
round-nosed (snug-nosed) pliers
medium decorative glass beads in
yellow, green, silver and clear
pencil
small glass rocaille beads and square
beads in complementary shades
pair of glass candlesticks

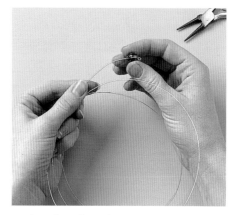

1 Cut four lengths of wire, each 1m/ 40in long for every candlestick. Bend a loop at the end of the first length with round-nosed (snug-nosed) pliers and thread on a decorative bead.

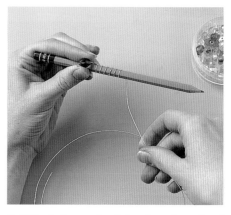

2 Wind the end of the first length of wire around a pencil six times to form a spiral. Make sure you leave some space between the coils, for threading more beads.

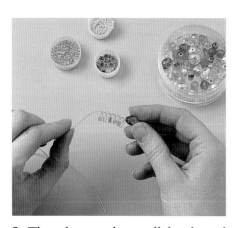

3 Thread on eight small beads and divide them along the spiral. Thread on a medium-sized bead and repeat, forming spirals and threading beads until you reach the end of the wire. At the end, twist the wire with pliers.

4 Thread on the final decorative bead and finish with a loop at the end of the wire. Make up the other three spirals in the same way, distributing the beads evenly along the spiral.

5 Wrap two spiral lengths around the stem of each candlestick to form an interesting shape. Secure the spirals in place by binding them gently to the candlestick stem with more of the silver wire.

Magically crafted from a roll of wire, this delicate little chandelier was twisted and curled with long-nosed pliers. Hang the chandelier from a chain and hook so that it can twist in passing air currents.

Bent Wire Chandelier

you will need

roll of silver bonsai-training wire

wire cutters

ruler or tape measure

long-nosed pliers

roll of gardening wire

4 self-tapping screws and screwdriver

glue gun with all-purpose glue sticks

4 drawing pins (thumb tacks)

4 night-lights

large sequins

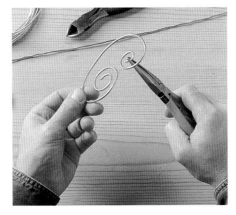

1 Cut a 35cm/13¾in length of bonsai wire to make the first kidney-shaped curl. Hold the wire with your free hand and, gripping the end with the long-nosed pliers, shape it into a curl. Then, holding the first curl in your hand, curl the other end.

2 Make a single curl from a smaller piece of wire. Make two more single curls. Each branch is made of three single curls and one kidney-shaped curl. There are four branches on the chandelier in total.

3 With wire cutters cut a 12cm/4¾in length of gardening wire and use it to bind the kidney-shaped curl and two of the single curls together at the point, as shown. Wind the wire round like a spring to make a neat binding.

4 Screw a self-tapping screw into the centre of the binding, leaving at least 12mm/½in protruding at the top.

5 Bind the third single curl on to the back of the kidney shape, winding a length of gardening wire into a neat binding as before. ▶

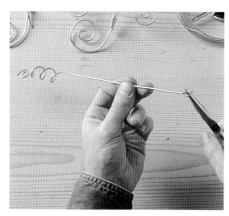

6 Use the wire cutters to neatly snip off the end of the gardening wire at an angle, close to the binding. Repeat the above steps to make the remaining three branches of the chandelier.

7 Cut a 50cm/20in length of bonsai wire for the central column. Twist one end into a decorative spiral and the other into a small hook, as shown. The hook is used for hanging the chandelier from the ceiling.

8 Make two small, tight curls and bind them into the top end of the column, facing inwards. Bind the four branches on to the central column, with the open side of the kidney-shaped curls facing upwards.

9 Heat the glue gun, apply a dot of glue to one of the screwheads and immediately sit a drawing pin on it, point upwards. Repeat with the three remaining screwheads.

10 Press a night-light down on to each of the points of the drawing pins. Thread the large sequins on to the curls. Take care not to overdo this, as too many could detract from the elegance of the wire twists.

Create this splendid chandelier to hang over your dining table. The length of aluminium wire needed for this project is difficult to work with in the early stages.

Filigree Chandelier

you will need

permanent marker pen

ruler or tape measure

gloves

soft aluminium wire, 3mm/¹⁄₈in and 1mm/¹⁄₂₅in thick

round-nosed (snug-nosed) pliers

paper

wire cutters

5 glasses or jars at least 5.5cm/2¹⁄₄in in diameter

1 glass or jar at least 6cm/2¹⁄₂in in diameter

6 bath-plug chains

metal ring

1 Using a permanent marker pen and a ruler and wearing gloves, mark the 3mm/¹⁄₈in aluminium wire at 54.5cm/21½in and 5cm/2in. Repeat another four times, then mark a final point 5cm/2in further on. Using round-nosed (snug-nosed) pliers, bend each 5cm/2in section of wire into a loop, leaving the last 5cm/2in straight for joining. Weave the longer sections over and under each other to form a star shape.

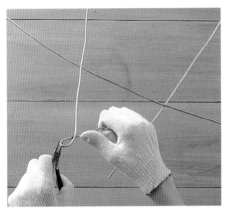

2 Bind the last 5cm/2in to the start of the wire, using the finer wire. Bind each loop closed.

3 To even up the star shape, divide each 54.5cm/21½in length of wire into three equal sections of just over 18cm/7in, and mark the points. Match up the marks where the wires cross and bind them together at these points using 1mm/¹⁄₂₅in wire.

4 Enlarge the templates provided at the back of the book. Cut 30 lengths of the thicker wire, 33cm/13in long. Using the round-nosed pliers, bend 15 of these around the nosed double-coil template. ▶

5 Enlarge the templates at the back of the book. Using round-nosed pliers, bend the remaining 15 lengths of wire around the templates to make five double coils, five arched double coils and five single-looped coils.

6 To create the glass holders, cut five lengths of the thicker wire each 50cm/20in. Wrap each wire around a jar twice and overlap the ends. Use the template to coil the wire at each end. To make the central glass holder, cut a 60cm/24in length of wire and wrap it three times around the larger glass or jar to make a plain coil.

7 Using five short lengths of the fine aluminium wire, bind the five double coils on to the central holder. Arrange the coils so that they are evenly placed and sit flat against the bottom of the plain coil. Trim any untidy wire ends carefully, using the wire cutters.

8 Bind the double coils together where the sides touch to make the raised central piece. Then bind the arched double coils and the single-looped coils around the edge of the double coils, alternating the two shapes. Bind the alternating shapes to each other, as well as to the double coils.

9 To each small glass holder, bind one nosed double coil to the coils on the glass holder and two to the ring. Place each structure inside the points of the frame so that the noses of the nosed double coils fit into the corners and the coils of the holder face towards the tip. Bind in place.

10 Bind the central piece to the star frame at all the points of contact. Attach a bath-plug chain to each of the five points where the frame wires cross. Attach the hooks at the ends of the chains to the metal ring and close up. Attach the sixth chain to the top of the metal ring for hanging. Place the glasses or jars in the holders.

Wire frameworks are essential to many flower arrangements and are usually intended to be unobtrusive, but this one is not only functional but decorative.

Flower Holder

you will need

dark green plastic-coated garden wire,
3mm/⅛in thick
ruler or tape measure
wire cutters
flat-nosed pliers
broom handle
spray can
galvanized wire, 0.5mm/⅕₀in thick
bowl
pebbles

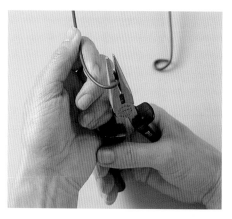

1 Cut eight lengths of garden wire each 90cm/35½in long to hold eight flower stems. Using flat-nosed pliers, turn a loop in each end of each length to hide the raw end of the wire.

2 Just below each loop, wrap one wire three times around a broom handle to form the stem supports. Repeat this process with the remaining seven lengths of wire.

3 Using the pliers, turn the stem through 90 degrees under each coil, and open out the coils a little. Create the final shape of the stem wire by wrapping it around a spray can. Vary the heights of the flower supports.

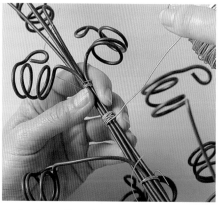

4 Gather all eight stems together and use fine galvanized wire to bind together the lower 8cm/3¼in of the straight sections. Adjust the curved sections so that they are regularly and pleasingly spaced.

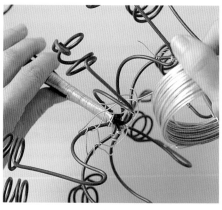

5 Weave the fine wire around the base curves and up the lower part of the flower supports to create a basket. Place the basket in a suitable bowl and weight it with a ring of pebbles. Add flowers of your choice.

This charming little shade is decorative rather than functional: so use a low wattage bulb, or hang a few together for maximum effect. The choice of paper defines the whole nature of the lampshade.

Flower Lampshade

you will need

copper wire, 1mm/¹⁄₂₅in and
0.5mm/¹⁄₅₀in thick
ruler or tape measure
wire cutters
handmade paper
PVA (white) glue
flame-retardant spray
pencil
scissors
towel
embroidery needle
flat-nosed pliers

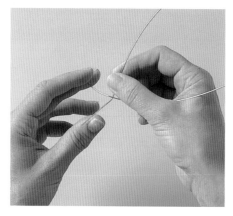

1 Cut a 40cm/16in length of 1mm/¹⁄₂₅in copper wire. Twist the two ends of the wire together for 12mm/½in, then pull the loop into a petal shape to match the template at the back of the book. (For a larger flower, work with a 50cm/20in length of copper wire.)

2 Stiffen the paper with diluted PVA (white) glue. Allow to dry completely, then spray the paper with flame-retardant spray. When dry, place the wire petal shape on the paper and draw around it. Cut out the petal, then place it on a towel and use an embroidery needle to punch fine holes around the edge.

3 Cut a 50cm/20in length of 0.5mm/¹⁄₅₀in copper wire and mark the centre. Starting at the petal tip, thread the wire through the first hole and pull it through as far as the centre mark. Sew the petal to the frame. Twist the ends together and trim. Make six petals.

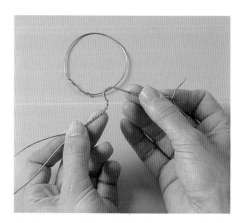

4 Cut a 25cm/10in length of the thicker wire and form a 6cm/2½in diameter circle. Cut two 20cm/8in lengths and twist them together for 10cm/4in in the centre. Form a half-loop in the middle, following the template as a guide.

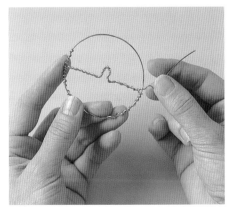

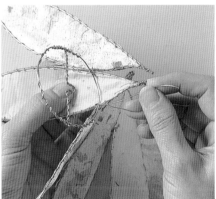

5 Attach the looped rod by winding the untwisted ends of the wire around the circle, to form a frame for the petals, and to enable you to hang the lampshade securely from the electric cable.

6 Join the petals in a row by threading the finer wire through a punched hole on each side of each petal 4cm/1½in from the top, then twisting and trimming the ends.

7 Attach the petals to the circle in the same way, passing the fine wire through the same hole. Once all of the petals are joined, bend the tops and splay the bottoms of the petals to shape the flower.

Fashion a bunch of fabulous flowers, woven from richly coloured fuse wire. This wire comes in many colours, so you can add the leaves and tendrils by spiralling and coiling the thicker and darker wires.

Fused Flowers

you will need

enamelled copper wire in two colours, 1mm/¹⁄₂₅in and 0.8mm/¹⁄₃₁in thick

ruler or tape measure

wire cutters

hand drill

round-nosed (snug-nosed) pliers

1 Cut six 50cm/20in lengths of the thicker enamelled copper wire. Twist them together along half the length using a hand drill to form the stem. Bend back the wires loosely.

2 Holding the wires in one hand, attach a length of the finer wire to the centre. Start weaving over and under the six wires.

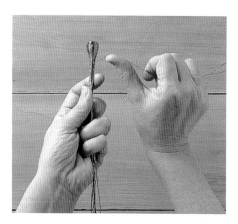

3 Weave a bulb-shaped stamen, 2.5cm/1in high and 1.5cm/³⁄₅in wide. Bend each of the wires back up around the woven stamen between your finger and thumb.

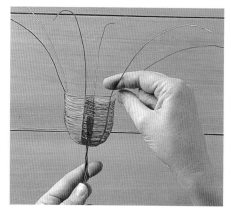

4 Using a different-coloured wire, weave a flower shape 6cm/2½in high.

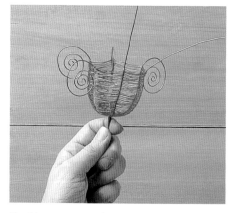

5 Using round-nosed (snug-nosed) pliers, bend each remaining length of wire to form a loose coil. Finally, bind the stem with several lengths of fine enamelled copper wire.

This is an effective way to create a magical container for a night-light. When the candle is lit it looks like a treasure pile and gives a warm, sparkling light as a room decoration or on the table.

Jewel Night-light

you will need

silver-plated wire, 1.5mm/^{1}/19in and 0.8mm/^{1}/31in thick

ruler or tape measure

wire cutters

large rolling pin

75 round glass beads, 14mm/^{5}/8in

75 silver-plated bead cages, 14mm/^{5}/8in

flat-nosed pliers

wooden spoon

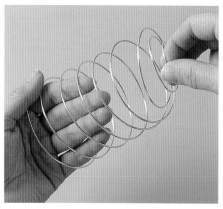

1 Cut a 165cm/65in length of the thicker silver-plated wire and coil it around a large rolling pin to make the frame. Slide the coil off the rolling pin and ease it apart a little. At one end, shape the frame into a cone by making the loops slightly smaller. Pull up the last few loops so that they sit upright.

2 To put the glass beads inside the wire cages, pull each cage slightly apart and slip in a bead. The colours of the beads used can obviously be varied to suit your colour scheme, but simple combinations of two complementary shades, as used here, work well.

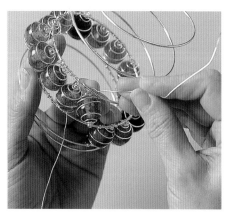

3 Leaving a loop of wire at the base for stability, begin binding the caged beads between the second and third loops, using the fine wire. Pull the wire tight as you work, using pliers. Work around the loops until you reach the point where the coils are twisted upright. There are four rows of beads.

4 Wrap a 115cm/45in length of the thicker wire around the handle of a wooden spoon. Slide the coil off the handle, then flatten it. Join the ends with fine wire to form the circular base. Bind the base to the bottom of the frame with fine wire at three separate points.

5 Finally, thread a length of fine wire through the middle of a bead and attach it to the top of the frame, where the coils are twisted upright. Wrap the wire around the coils several times to secure the bead to the top of the structure.

This jazzy coloured, beaded bottle makes the perfect container for salad dressings or olive oil. Its unique cover is made from the fine wires found inside a telephone cable.

Fiesta Oil Bottle

you will need
3m/10ft length of 6-pair telephone cable
empty thread reels
double-sided adhesive tape
scissors
quarter-size wine bottle
ruler or tape measure
small glass beads in two contrasting colours
a few larger glass beads
wire cutters
all-purpose instant glue

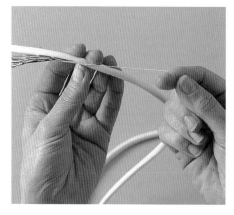

1 To extract the thin coloured wires from the cable, pull the white cotton strand to strip back the coating. Remove the wires, untwist them and roll each colour on to an empty reel. Choose six colours.

2 Cut thin strips of double-sided tape and stick them down firmly in two lines on opposite sides of the quarter-size wine bottle. Make sure the top strip starts directly under the screw top.

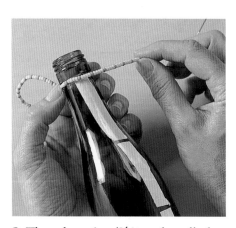

3 Thread on 6cm/2½ in of small glass beads, using alternate colours. Form a loop. Attach the loop to the bottle by twisting the wire back on itself. Thread on more beads to make a circle around the neck of the bottle.

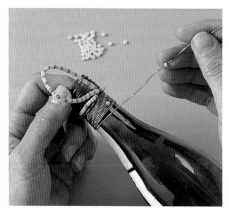

4 Wind the remaining length of coloured wire around the bottle, threading on the odd small bead as you go. The adhesive tape will hold the wire in place.

5 To attach each new colour of wire, use a larger bead. Thread both wire ends through the bead and then pull them downwards.

6 Press the wire ends flat against the bottle and trim the ends neatly. Wind the new colour around the bottle as before, covering the loose ends.

7 Continue to wind the coloured wires down the length of the bottle, attaching new colours as you go. Attach a few larger beads when you reach the main body of the bottle.

8 When you reach the bottom of the bottle, thread another row of beads on to the last length of wire and glue this all round the bottle using all-purpose instant glue.

Aluminium wire is light and easy to bend, but a group of these twisted candlesticks makes a substantial centrepiece. The skill in making them lies in plaiting (braiding) the aluminium wire evenly.

Classic Candlesticks

you will need

aluminium wire, 3mm/¹⁄₈in and 1.5mm/¹⁄₁₉in thick

ruler or tape measure

wire cutters

coloured copper wire, 0.8mm/¹⁄₃₁in thick

round-nosed (snug-nosed) pliers

glass beads

candle

2 pencils

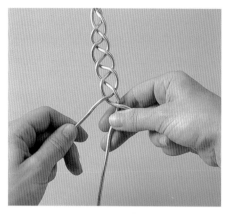

1 Cut three equal lengths of 3mm/¹⁄₈in aluminium wire. These should be 45cm/18in for the small, 50cm/20in for the medium and 55cm/22in for the tall candlestick. Bind the three pieces together 10cm/4in from the top using coloured copper wire, then plait (braid) them together.

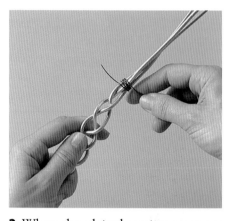

2 When the plaited section measures 10cm/4in, 15cm/6in or 18cm/7in, depending on the size of candlestick you have chosen to make, bind the three wire pieces together with the coloured copper wire, as at the top. The binding should be directly under the plaited section.

3 Separate the three wires beneath the binding and shape into legs, bending each wire up and then down to make a double curve. Use round-nosed (snug-nosed) pliers to curl each end into a loop, which must be equal in height, and add a bead.

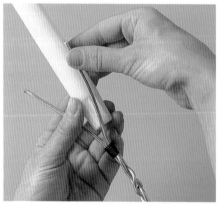

4 Open out the wires at the top of the candlestick, then position a candle between the wires and mould them around it.

5 Cut a 1.5m/59in length of 1.5mm/¹⁄₁₉in aluminium wire and fold it in half. Loop a pencil into each end of the doubled wire and twist, using the pencils as handles. Cut a 75cm/30in length of coloured wire and wind it over the twisted aluminium.

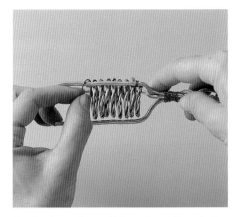

6 Coil a 50cm/20in length of the twisted wire gently around the candle base, then bind this coil inside the shaped spikes with a few turns of coloured wire at the top and bottom of each spike.

7 To complete the candlestick, use round-nosed pliers to curl the spikes down into three loops.

Delicate coils of pale galvanized wire make an ornate candle holder to hang on the wall. Enlarge the template to the size required, then place the wire coils over it as you bend them to check that they match.

Swirled Candle Sconce

you will need

paper

pencil

wire cutters

galvanized wire, 2mm/¹∕₁₃in thick

ruler or tape measure

long-nosed pliers

fine galvanized wire

clear adhesive tape

candle

1 Enlarge the template at the back of the book to the finished size and draw it on a piece of paper. Cut the 2mm/ ¹∕₁₃in wire into two lengths of 30cm/ 12in for the top hanger and lower coil; one of 50cm/20in for the centre piece; four of 55cm/21½in for the side pieces; and one of 80cm/32in for the candle holder.

2 Using pliers, bend each length to fit the relevant coiled shape on the sconce design. It may help to have a second photocopy of the design, so that you can position each length as soon as you have shaped it.

3 Take the top hanger piece and wind the fine wire around the crossover point, trim the wire and take the ends to the back of the sconce.

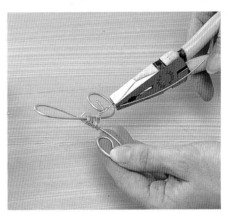

4 Turn the shape over and twist the ends of the fine wire together securely, then clip off any excess. Use this method for all the seams described.

▶

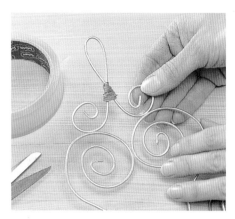

5 Secure two of the side pieces under the hanger with tabs of adhesive tape at the points indicated. This tape will hold the coils steady while you make the wire seams.

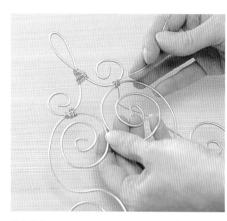

6 Make strong wire seams at the taped points using fine wire.

7 Tape the centre piece into position between the two side pieces, then wind the fine wire around the small round shape in the centre, securing it to the side pieces.

8 Tape the other pieces into place and make small wire seams to secure them, winding a short piece of fine wire around three times. Secure the ends of the fine wire by twisting them together at the back.

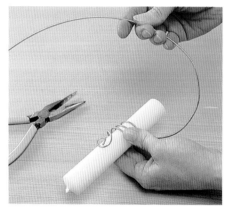

9 Make the candle holder with the remaining length of 2mm/¹⁄₁₃in wire. Begin with a small spiral, then wind the wire around the candle about five times, as shown.

10 Bend the end of the wire under the coil across the base (the base of the candle will rest on this), and then into an elongated hook shape at the back. Hook the holder on to the sconce and wire securely in place.

An African toy was the inspiration for this project. Handmade from wire and scrap materials, it was ingeniously designed so that a little figure pedals a bicycle when the toy is pushed along.

Bicycle Toy

you will need

galvanized wire, 1.5mm/¹⁄₁₉in thick

ruler or tape measure

wire cutters

permanent marker pens

bottle

parallel (channel-type) pliers

twisty wire tape in two colours

cotton reel

coloured pipe cleaners

small cardboard tube

paper clips (fasteners)

selection of large and small wooden beads

strong glue

ribbon

doll's straw hat

fabric in two colours

scissors

needle and thread

double-sided adhesive tape

freezer-bag ties

doll's basket

silk flowers

green bamboo cane

1 To make the bicycle, cut a 1m/40in length of galvanized wire. Mark the wire at intervals of 5cm/2in, 31cm/12¼in, 5cm/2in, 3cm/1¼in, 2cm/¾in, 2cm/¾in, 4cm/1½in, 2cm/¾in, 2cm/¾in, 3cm/1¼in, 5cm/2in, 31cm/12¼in and 5cm/2in. Wrap both 31cm/12¼in sections around a bottle with a diameter of approximately 10cm/4in to form the wheels. Using pliers, bend in the 5cm/2in at each end of the wire to form a radius.

2 Bend in the other two 5cm/2in sections into the centre of the wheel. Make the bicycle pedals by bending right angles in the wire at the marked points. Bend each wheel so that it is at a right angle to the pedals.

3 Transfer the twisty wire tape to a cotton reel to make it easier to handle. Bind tape around the wheel, along the radius, across the pedals and around the second wheel.

▶

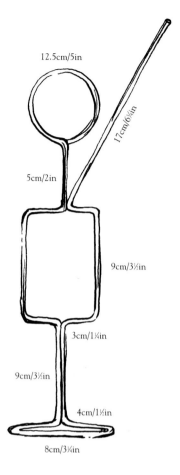

12.5cm/5in

5cm/2in

17cm/6¾in

9cm/3½in

3cm/1¼in

9cm/3½in

4cm/1½in

8cm/3¼in

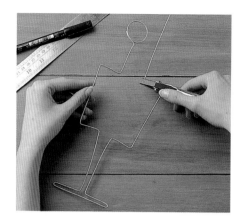

4 To make the bicycle body, cut a 1m/40in length of galvanized wire and mark it at intervals of 12.5cm/5in, 5cm/2in, 3cm/1¼in, 9cm/3½in, 3cm/1¼in, 9cm/3½in, 4cm/1½in, 8cm/3¼in, 4cm/1½in, 9cm/3½in, 3cm/1¼in, 9cm/3½in, 3cm/1¼in, 17cm/6¾in. Cut off any excess and follow the diagram to shape the bicycle. Bend the 12.5cm/5in section into a circle to form the seat.

5 Bend up the handlebars, seat and stick at right angles. Bind wire tape in another colour all around the handlebars, leaving a tiny gap near each end for the doll's hands. Bind the handlebar neck and the frame. Halfway along, bind to the wheel. Bind the seat, leaving the stick bare. Continue binding the frame, binding on the other wheel. The wheels should rotate.

6 To make the doll's body, twist together the ends of two pipe cleaners. Make a hole at either side of the top and bottom of the cardboard tube. Thread the pipe cleaners through the top holes for the arms. For the upper legs, bend two more pipe cleaners in half and twist the ends together. Loosely attach to the bottom holes with a paper clip (fastener).

7 Using a permanent marker pen draw a face on a large, plain bead. Make a hole in the tube end. Thread a pipe cleaner through the hole. Thread on a small bead for the neck and then the large bead. Bend the pipe cleaner over the top of the head and over the bottom edge of the tube so that the head is held on securely.

8 Bend two pipe cleaners in half to make the lower legs and thread through the upper legs. Wrap a brown pipe cleaner around the bottom of each leg and bend up to make the doll's shoes. Glue three brown pipe cleaners on to the top of the head and plait (braid) on each side to make the hair. Tie a ribbon on to the end of each plait. Glue on a doll's hat.

9 Cut a 10cm/4in square of fabric and fray. Cut a slit from one corner to the centre to make the shawl. Cut a 10 × 33cm/4 × 13in rectangle from another fabric. Sew a line of running stitch along the top edge and then gather to make the skirt. Wrap a piece of strong double-sided tape around the doll's body. Dress the doll and tie a length of ribbon around the waist.

10 Attach the doll's feet to the pedals with freezer-bag ties. Wrap each arm around the handlebars, twisting the excess length around the arm. Place a little basket over one arm first and fill it with silk flowers.

◀ **11** Apply strong glue to the piece of wire projecting from the bicycle seat and insert into the hollow centre of a green bamboo cane. Allow the glue to dry. Apply glue to the top end of the cane and slide on two or three beads to make a handle. Toddlers' beads are best for this as they have large holes.

Practical

Wire Objects

In addition to creating beautiful and decorative objects for around the home, you can use wire to create all manner of useful, practical items. You can twist and sculpt wire to make an enormous variety of holders and dishes for the bathroom and kitchen, as well as creating attractive containers for bottles and glasses, and building strong racks and shelves for storing all those essential items needed in every home.

Coil and Weave

Wire is one of the most useful materials to have in the home as it has a wide variety of functional uses. Where would we be without wire coat hangers or metal hooks? In this chapter, wire is used to make a selection of practical but decorative objects for the home, ranging from toothbrush holders and soap dishes for the bathroom, toast racks and shelves for the kitchen, to a wire bird feeder for the garden.

Wire is extremely practical. It is easy to use. Thicker gauges, once woven together, are strong and capable of supporting a heavy weight, and are usually rustproof, making wire ideal for use in bathrooms and kitchens. What's more, it is easy to clean, and hard to break.

Galvanized wire is used in this chapter to sculpt items, and to provide a

framework over which a flimsier material can be wrapped. Wire coat hangers can be recycled for small-scale projects that still require strength. Gardening wire is ideal to use outdoors; its plastic coating means that it does not tarnish. Another

wire worth using is tinned copper wire; this has a lovely colour and, again, does not tarnish. Chicken wire has a range of practical uses, both indoor and outdoor, and even food and drinks cans may be given an imaginative new function.

Wire is an attractive material in its own right and needs little adornment. Its clean and functional appearance complements a stainless steel kitchen. A wire trivet, toast rack and utility rack would look ideal in a more modern kitchen with minimal decor

and clean unfussy surfaces. For functional items, simplicity is the important factor. Decorative motifs and curlicues are unnecessary and detract from the finished piece. Keep edges straight and neat for the best effect.

Many of the wire items featured in this chapter can also be made as gifts for friends and family. Handmade items are always treasured. If you make a project as a gift, try to personalize it somehow, perhaps by incorporating a monogram in the design.

These monogrammed clothes hangers make lovely gifts, or a charming gesture in a guest's bedroom. The instructions show how to make the hanger as well as the decoration.

Monogrammed Clothes Hanger

you will need

galvanized wire, 2mm/¹⁄₁₃in, 1mm/¹⁄₂₅in and 0.3mm/¹⁄₈₃in thick

ruler or tape measure

wire cutters

large pliers

beads

round-nosed (snug-nosed) pliers

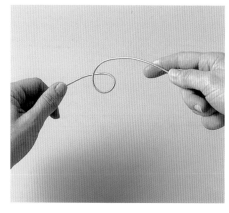

1 Cut a 140cm/55in length of the 2mm/¹⁄₁₃in galvanized wire. Bend it to form a loop 25cm/10in from one end, as shown.

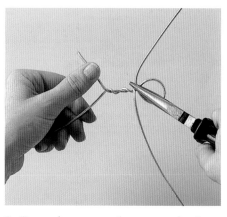

2 Cross the two ends over at the loop and, holding them at the crossing-point with pliers, twist the two ends together for 5cm/2in.

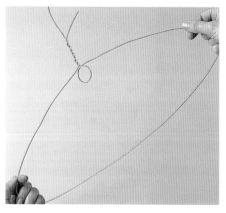

3 Above the twist, trim off the short end and shape the longer end to form the hook. Holding the circle of wire with the hook at the top, pull out the sides to form the hanger shape.

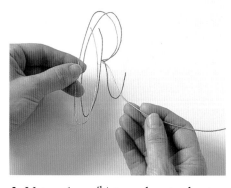

4 Using 1mm/¹⁄₂₅in galvanized wire, shape the initial letter for the centre of the hanger following the relevant template from the alphabet at the back of the book.

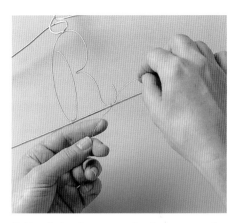

5 Bind the letter to the hanger at the top and bottom using the 0.3mm/⅛₃in galvanized wire.

6 With 1mm/¹⁄₂₅in wire, make the decorative shapes using the templates at the back of the book as a guide. Thread beads on to the ends of the wires, then twist into shape using round-nosed (snug-nosed) pliers.

7 Attach the shapes to the main frame in the order of the numbers shown on the template. Bind each one to the top and bottom of the hanger, using fine wire as before.

This unusual fly swatter is simple to make and extremely effective. It is designed to resemble a giant flower, and is an attractive addition to the kitchen or conservatory.

Flower Fly Swatter

you will need

straightened wire coat hanger

wire cutters

pliers

broom handle

ruler or tape measure

wooden ball, 2.5cm/1in diameter

paper

pencil

plastic mesh

scissors

cotton knitting yarn

needle

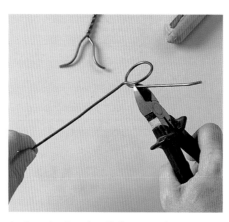

1 Cut the hook off the coat hanger. To form the flower centre, using pliers, bend one end of the wire and form a loop using a broom handle to bend the wire around. Trim.

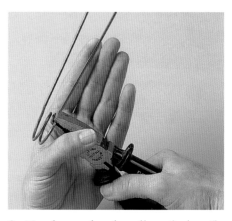

2 To form the handle of the fly swatter, measure down 45cm/18in from the top of the loop and bend a 90° angle. Turn this end around the broom handle twice, then bend at 90° again and cut off, leaving a 4cm/1½in length parallel with the stem. Twist the end of the wire around the stem. Open the double loop and insert the wooden ball.

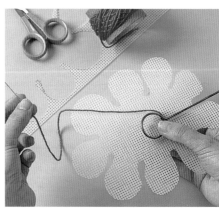

3 Enlarge the flower template at the back of the book to the required size. Trace it on to the plastic mesh, and cut out neatly. Centre the top loop of the wire stem on the flower shape and oversew firmly in place with cotton yarn.

Made from galvanized wire, this practical yet decorative accessory for the kitchen will co-ordinate with any style of kitchen decor. You could make a set of trivets in different shapes and sizes.

Heart-shaped Trivet

you will need
galvanized wire, 2mm/¹⁄₁₃in thick
wire cutters
ruler or tape measure
broom handle
pliers

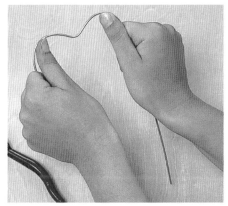

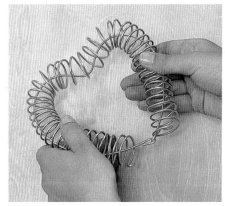

1 Cut a 50cm/20in length of wire, and form it into a heart shape by bending the wire in the centre to form the dip in the top of the heart. At the ends, make hooks to join the two ends of the wire together.

2 Make a coil by tightly and evenly wrapping more wire round a broom handle 50 times. Make hooks in the ends in the same way as before.

3 Thread the coil over the heart. Connect the ends of the heart by crimping the hooked ends together with pliers. Manipulate the coil, to make it sit evenly around the heart, before joining and crimping the ends together with pliers.

Transform a wire coat hanger into this charming toilet-tissue holder. Hearts are a traditional motif in folk-art designs, and transform the most functional of objects into personal works of art.

Toilet-tissue Holder

you will need
wire coat hanger
wire cutters
parallel (channel-type) pliers
piece of wood
drill
screw and screwdriver
ruler or tape measure
permanent marker pen
general-purpose pliers
galvanized wire, 0.8mm/¹⁄₃₁in thick

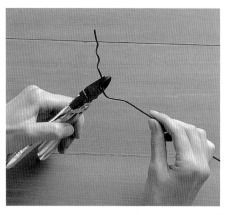

1 Open out the coat hanger hook and cut off the hook and the twisted wire with wire cutters. Straighten the wire using parallel (channel-type) pliers.

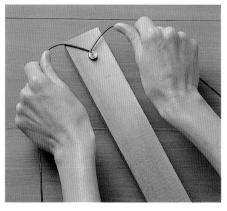

2 Drill a hole in a piece of wood and insert a screw. Wrap the wire around the screw halfway along its length. The screw will hold the wire firmly. Mould the wire into a heart shape.

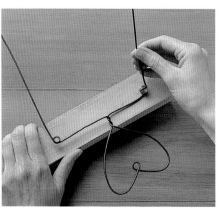

3 Allow 6.5cm/2½in between the eye and the bottom of the heart. Twist the wires together twice at the bottom of the heart. Bend out the remaining wires at right angles. Unscrew the wire heart and replace the screw in the piece of wood. Measure 6.5cm/2½in from the bottom of the heart along each wire, then wrap each wire once around the screw at this point and bend up the end at a right angle.

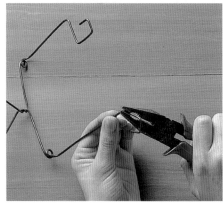

4 Using a marker pen, mark each remaining length of wire at intervals of 7.5cm/3in, 3cm/1¼in, 3cm/1¼in, 2cm/⅘in and 2cm/⅘in. Bend the wire into right angles at the marked points using general-purpose pliers, so the ends that will hold the toilet tissue point inwards. To decorate, loosely wrap a length of 0.8mm/¹⁄₃₁in galvanized wire around the whole of the structure.

Extremely useful, bottle carriers can be quite hard to find. This version is made from thick galvanized wire formed into a clover leaf shape and holds three bottles.

Bottle Carrier

you will need

galvanized gardening wire, 2mm/$\frac{1}{13}$in and 0.8mm/$\frac{1}{31}$in thick

ruler or tape measure

wire cutters

bottle

general-purpose pliers

permanent marker pen

nail, 5mm/$\frac{1}{5}$in long

large wooden bead

strong glue

hammer

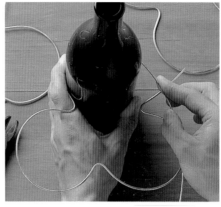

1 Cut three 80cm/32in lengths of the thicker wire. Leave 10cm/4in at one end of each wire and wrap the next section around a bottle. At the point of overlap, bend back the wire to form a second, then a third curve. Make a loop at each end of the wire and close together. Cut off any excess wire. Make two more clover shapes.

2 Cut seven 80cm/32in and two 91.5cm/36in lengths of thicker wire. Bundle them together so that the longest are in the centre and stick out at one end. This end forms the handle. Starting where the longer wires stick out, bind the bundle with thin wire for 42cm/16½in. To form the base of the bottle carrier, divide the wires into groups of three. Bend each group away from the central shaft at right angles. Arrange the wires in each group side by side. Measure 3cm/1¼in from the handle and bind together for 2cm/⅘in. Bend out the outer two wires at right angles. Measure 5cm/2in from the bound section and mark each wire. Bend each wire up at a right angle so that it stands parallel to the handle. Make a hook at the end of each wire.

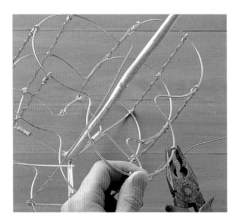

3 Slot the three clover shapes into the structure, and then close up the hooks around the top clover shape. Bind the bottom clover in place. Bind up each strut, securing the middle clover shape halfway up. Bind over the wire ends at the top of the structure.

4 Wrap a length of 2mm/$\frac{1}{13}$in wire around the nail to make a coil. Thread the bead on to the wires at the top of the central shaft. Apply strong glue to the coil and hammer on the bead.

This clever little device made of two recycled coat hangers will give your rolling pin its own place on the kitchen wall, looking decorative as well as being out of the way.

Rolling Pin Holder

you will need

galvanized wire, 2mm/$\frac{1}{13}$in thick

wire cutters

ruler or tape measure

screwdriver

pliers

fine brass picture-hanging wire

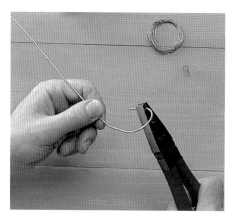

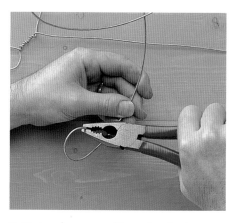

1 Cut two 75cm/30in lengths of the galvanized wire. Find the middle of one length and then bend it around a screwdriver handle to make a loop. Twist the two halves six times.

2 Using the pliers, curl the two ends of the wire forwards. The curls form the handle that holds the rolling pin, so check the fit as you work.

3 Twist the second length of wire into a heart shape – bend it sharply in the middle, then bring the ends down in opposite directions so that they cross over. Curl the ends.

4 Using short lengths of brass picture-hanging wire, bind the two lengths together at the points shown. Place your rolling pin between the curled hooks to judge the width needed.

The design for this whimsical egg tree derives from eastern European folk art. The basket at the bottom is traditionally used for bread. Tinned copper wire has been used – it is malleable but does not tarnish.

Decorative Egg Tree

you will need

ruler or tape measure

tinned copper wire, 2mm/$\frac{1}{13}$in and 1mm/$\frac{1}{25}$in thick

rolling pin

wire cutters

permanent marker pen

pencil

tacking wire

general-purpose pliers

strong tape

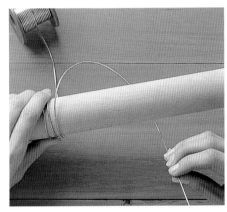

1 Measure 60cm/24in of 2mm/$\frac{1}{13}$in wire but do not cut off. Beginning at this point, wrap this section of wire three times around a rolling pin. Remove from the rolling pin and grip the middle of the final loop between your thumb and forefinger.

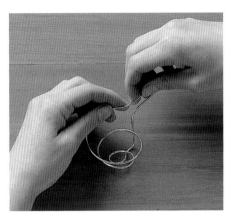

2 Wrap the loop around your thumb and then pull it down. The second loop will reduce in diameter. The loops form the egg holder. Bend the remaining end of wire up the outside of the egg holder to meet the wire still attached to the spool.

3 Bend both wires away from the egg holder to make the branch. Bind the two branch wires together for 7.5cm/ 3in using the thinner wire. Trim the thinner wire, leaving 2cm/$\frac{4}{5}$in free. Bend the branch wires down at a right angle. Measure 60cm/24in of the branch wire from the spool and trim.

4 Make ten more egg holders. The bound section of the six lower holders measures 7.5cm/3in, and the section for the five upper holders measures 4cm/1$\frac{1}{2}$in.

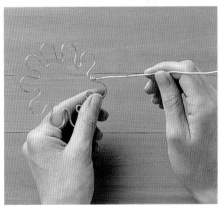

5 Measure 6.5cm/2$\frac{1}{2}$in of 2mm/$\frac{1}{13}$in wire and mark the point. Wrap the next section ten times around a pencil to form petals. Bend these round to form a flower. Use the first 6.5cm/ 2$\frac{1}{2}$in of wire to join the flower and cut off. Bend down the remaining wire at a right angle. Cut at 76cm/30in. ▶

6 Form the top egg holder by measuring another 60cm/24in piece of 2mm/ 1/13in wire, without cutting off. As before, begin at this point and wrap the section three times around the rolling pin. Remove from the rolling pin and wrap the first loop around your thumb and pull down. Measure 70cm/27½in and cut off the wire from the spool.

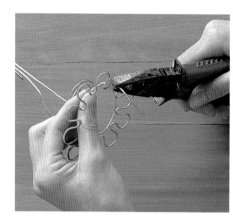

7 Bind the end of the top egg holder on to the flower, opposite the joint. To hold the wires in place while you are working, bind them together with tacking wire. Bend the long wire extending from the flower to curve down the outside of the spiral. Using 1mm/1/25in wire, start binding the two stem wires tightly together. Bind for 7cm/2¾in.

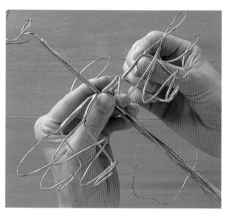

8 Bunch the stem wires of the upper five egg holders around the two stem wires to form the trunk. Wrap with a piece of strong tape to keep them in place. Using 1mm/1/25in wire, start binding the trunk from just below the point at which the egg holders join the stem. Bind the trunk for 7cm/ 2¾in. Then bind on the six lower egg holders. Bind the trunk for 25cm/10in below this second tier.

9 To make the basket, cut six lengths of 2mm/1/13in wire measuring 91cm/ 36in, 90cm/35½in, 89cm/35in, 76cm/ 30in, 66cm/26in and 46cm/18in. Using pliers, bend hooks at both ends of each wire. Form each length into a ring and hook the two ends together. Squeeze the hooks together using pliers to close.

10 Splay out the wires from the base of the egg tree and curve upwards to form the side struts of the basket. Check that the diameter at the top is the same as that of the largest ring.

11 Tack the rings on to the struts. Start with the smallest at the bottom and work up to the largest at the top. Allow 2.5cm/1in between each ring. Attach the largest ring by wrapping the ends of the strut wires around it. The basket should be about 9cm/ 3½in in height. Finally, bind the rings on to the struts.

This intriguing little basket is made using a simple wrapping technique. The tightly woven pipe cleaners give a softness that is irresistible to touch. Use this basket to hold jewellery.

Woven Pipe Cleaner Basket

you will need

galvanized wire, 1.5mm/¹⁄₁₉in and 0.5mm/¹⁄₅₀in thick

ruler or tape measure

wire cutters

50 lilac and 24 grey pipe cleaners, 30cm/12in long

flat-nosed pliers

round-nosed (snug-nosed) pliers

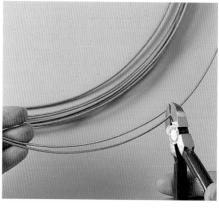

1 For the struts of the basket, measure and cut eight lengths of 1.5mm/¹⁄₁₉in galvanized wire, each 36cm/14in. Retain the curve of the wire as you cut the lengths from the coil. Cut one 30cm/12in length of the 0.5mm/¹⁄₅₀in galvanized wire.

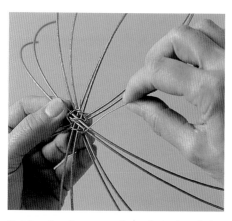

2 Use the fine wire length to bind the struts together at the centre. Bind two pairs together at right angles, then place the remaining pairs diagonally. Wind the fine wire around all the individual struts to hold them in position, evenly spaced.

3 Weave a lilac pipe cleaner over the centre of the basket so that all the fine wire is covered.

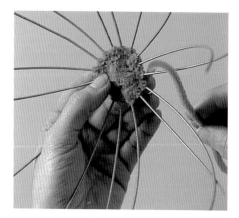

4 Take the pipe cleaner under each wire, back around it and then on to the next, pushing the pipe cleaners in towards the centre to keep the weave tight. Adjust the wires as necessary to keep the shape and spacing even. Work in lilac until the woven piece measures 7.5cm/3in.

5 When you reach the end of a pipe cleaner or want to use a different colour, join the lengths by bending a small hook in the end of each. Hook them together and flatten the hooks with flat-nosed pliers.

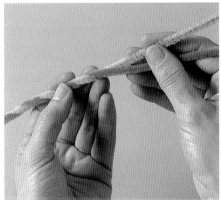

6 Work two rows of weaving in the grey pipe cleaners, then three lilac, two grey, four lilac, two grey, five lilac, and four grey, to bring you to the top edge of the basket.

7 Take two lilac pipe cleaners and hook them together, and do the same with two grey pipe cleaners. Hold the two colours together at one end and twist them firmly together. Join the twisted length to the last grey length on the basket and arrange it around the top edge, outside the struts.

8 Trim the tops of the struts to 5mm/⅕in and use round-nosed (snug-nosed) pliers to bend them over the edging. Weave the ends of the twisted edge into its beginning.

These ingenious containers look like fat little pots, but are actually made of brightly coloured fabric stretched over wire frames. Use them as containers for cotton wool.

Fabric-covered Baskets

you will need
galvanized wire, 3mm/⅛in,
2mm/¹⁄₁₃in and 1mm/¹⁄₂₅in thick
ruler or tape measure
wire cutters
long-nosed pliers
masking tape
two-way stretch fabric
scissors
sewing machine
sewing thread
needle

1 Measure and cut three lengths of 3mm/⅛in galvanized wire 45cm/18in long. Cross the wires at the centres and bind together using 1mm/¹⁄₂₅in wire so that the six prongs splay out evenly in a star shape. Using 2mm/¹⁄₁₃in wire, make a double ring 13cm/5in in diameter and bind it centrally to the framework to form a base.

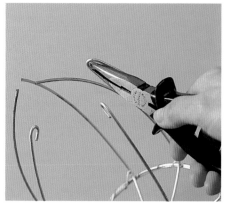

2 Use your fingers to bend each of the six prongs of the framework upwards where it joins the ring that forms the base. These prongs will form the structure for the sides of the container. Bend the end of each of the prongs into a tight loop using long-nosed pliers, as shown.

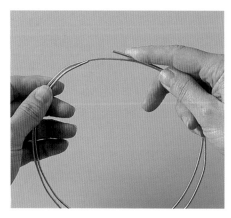

3 Make a second double ring of 2mm/¹⁄₁₃in wire to match the base, and then hold the two ends together temporarily using masking tape.

4 Slip the wire ring into the loops at the top of the framework, then bind in place using 1mm/¹⁄₂₅in wire.

5 Cut a 35cm/13¾in square of two-way stretch fabric. Fold in half and stitch down the long side to make a tube, using a machine stretch stitch.

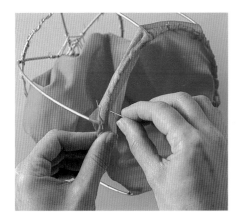

6 Place the fabric tube inside the wire framework. Hand stitch the raw edge to the top ring.

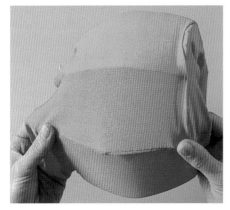

7 Pull the fabric up from inside the framework and carefully stretch it down around the outside of the tube. The fabric should be right side out.

8 Gather the raw edge under the base and stitch to the centre of the frame-work. Ease any remaining fabric up towards the top of the container, and secure it with curly clips made from galvanized wire.

An elegant wire cage will ensure that a ball of string is always there when you need it and that it never gets into a tangle. Easy to refill and attractive, this dispenser is a useful accessory for the potting shed.

Hanging String Dispenser

you will need

galvanized wire, 2mm/¹/₁₃in and 1mm/¹/₂₅in thick

ruler or tape measure

wire cutters

broom handle

ball of string

pliers

length of garden cane

pencil

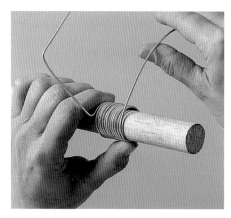

1 Cut a piece of 2mm/¹/₁₃in galvanized wire 1.7m/67in long. Bend a right angle about 30cm/12in from one end, then make 11 coils by turning the wire around a broom handle.

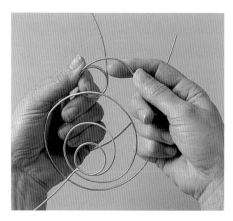

2 Loosen and spread the coils to form a shape that resembles a cone or half sphere. The shape needs to be large enough to fit loosely around the ball of string.

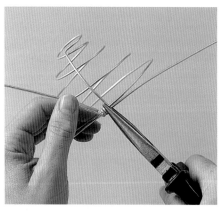

3 Bend the end of the wire down around the cone and use it to bind the last circle closed with pliers, leaving enough wire to create the feed loop for the string.

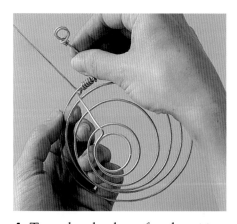

4 To make the loop for the string, wind a double coil around a garden cane about 2.5cm/1in along the remaining wire. Twist the end tightly around the stem and trim.

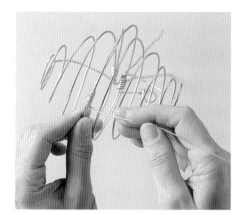

5 Make a second, matching cone, omitting the string loop. Using 1mm/$\frac{1}{25}$in wire, bind the two halves on the side opposite the loop.

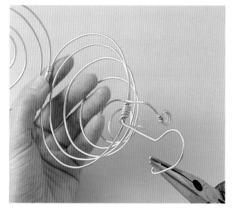

6 On each half, bend the free end of the wire at 90° to the circle and create two matching hanging hooks. Complete each hook with a tight loop at the end.

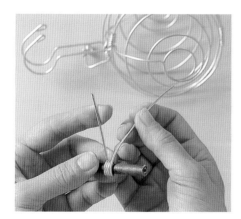

7 Cut a length of 2mm/$\frac{1}{13}$in wire and coil it several times around a pencil to make a closing ring for the dispenser. Trim and thread the ring over the hooks to keep the two halves shut.

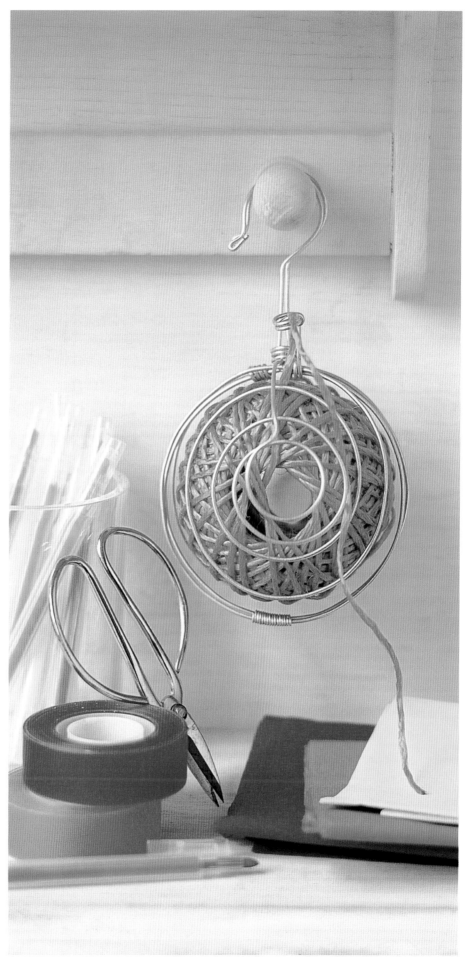

This sturdy basket is particularly suitable for gathering vegetables in from the garden. The mesh allows the soil to fall through and, because the wire is galvanized, the contents can be hosed down outside.

Wire Vegetable Basket

you will need

small-gauge chicken wire

wire cutters

gloves

ruler or tape measure

straining wire

galvanized wire, 1.5mm/$\frac{1}{19}$in and 0.8mm/$\frac{1}{31}$in thick

round-nosed (snug-nosed) pliers

permanent marker pen

tacking wire

broom handle

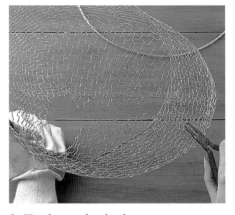

1 To make the cylinder, cut a piece of chicken wire 28 × 89cm/11 × 35in. Form it into an oval and join the short edges together. Cut a 94cm/37in length of straining wire and form it into an oval that will fit snugly inside the chicken-wire cylinder. Bind the ends together with the 0.8mm/$\frac{1}{31}$in galvanized wire.

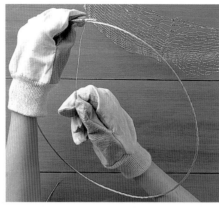

2 To shape the basket, count up ten holes from the bottom of the cylinder. This section will be the base. Use the round-nosed (snug-nosed) pliers to bend all the holes into heart shapes. To make the base support, cut a 70cm/28in length of straining wire and bind it into an oval.

3 Cut two 18cm/7in lengths and two 23cm/9in lengths of the 1.5mm/$\frac{1}{19}$in galvanized wire. Use round-nosed pliers to attach the wires to the oval to form a grid, binding where the wires cross.

4 Push the bottom edges of the basket together and bind with 0.8mm/$\frac{1}{31}$in galvanized wire to close up the base section neatly.

5 Position the base support on the bottom of the basket and bind it on to the chicken wire all the way around.

6 Place the large oval of straining wire inside the basket, 5cm/2in from the top. Fold the chicken wire over it, as shown. This will reinforce the top rim of the basket.

7 Mark a 54.5cm/21½in length of straining wire but do not cut it. Tack the end to one side of the basket and bend to form the handle. Secure the wire to the other side of the basket at the marked point. Wrap the next section of the straining wire around a broom handle to form ten loops. Bind these loops around the basket to the other side of the handle.

8 Bend the wire over the basket to double the handle. Bend the wire into a three-petalled decoration, as shown, and bind it to the basket. Loop the handle across again and make another three-petalled decoration on the other side.

9 Bend the wire back over the basket to form a fourth handle loop. Using the broom handle, make ten more loops in the wire and bind around the basket. Using 0.8mm/¹⁄₃₁in galvanized wire, bind the handle wires together, tucking the ends inside.

These semi-circular copper shelves have a Spanish style and will look good anywhere. The flattened coil edging adds strength to the framework as well as creating a shallow lip to stop anything from slipping off.

Decorative Shelves

you will need

paper

felt-tipped pen

ruler or tape measure

copper wire, 2mm/¹⁄₁₃in, 1.5mm/¹⁄₁₉in and 0.5mm/¹⁄₅₀in thick

wire cutters

flat-nosed pliers

round-nosed (snug-nosed) pliers

masking tape

30cm/12in length of wooden dowel, 1cm/²⁄₅in thick

2 picture hooks and nails

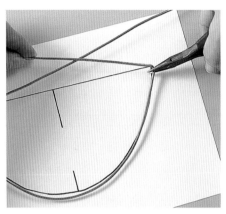

1 Enlarge the template at the back of the book to a width of 18cm/7in. Cut an 80cm/32in length of 2mm/¹⁄₁₃in copper wire and use the template as a guide to form the shelf frame. Use flat-nosed pliers to bend the wire, and start with the centre of the wire length at the centre front of the frame.

2 At the centre back, bend a right angle in the two ends of the wire so that they are vertical and parallel with each other. These will form the struts under the shelf. Using a pair of round-nosed (snug-nosed) pliers, turn each end of the wire to form a 5mm/¼in outward-facing hook.

3 Measure 6cm/2½in along the struts from the base and bend them out to the sides, so that the hooks meet the back corners of the base. Attach and firmly close the hooks.

4 Cut two 23cm/9in lengths of 2mm/¹⁄₁₃in wire and form a hook in one end of each. Attach these to the outer curved frame one-third of the way in from each side and close the hooks firmly. To hold them in place, wrap 0.5mm/¹⁄₅₀in wire along the front edge and around both hooks.

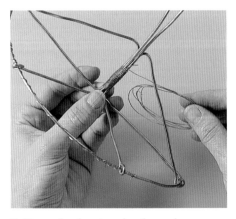

5 Bring both wires back to the centre back. Bend them up at right angles so that they run parallel to the central support wires. Cut a 150cm/59in length of 0.5mm/¹⁄₅₀in wire and bind the four wires together. Trim, leaving a 2.5cm/1in tail. Use pliers to tuck the end under the coils to secure it.

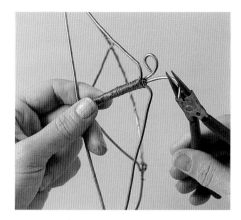

6 Trim the two ends at the bottom to 4cm/1½in and use round-nosed pliers to bend them into outward-facing loops which will lie flush with the wall.

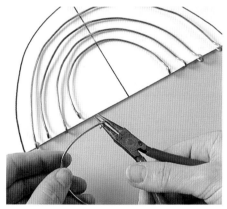

7 Make the wire hoops using 1.5mm/¹⁄₁₉in wire. Turn a hook in one end then bend the wire in a semi-circle 1cm/²⁄₅in in from the template edge and finish with a hook at the other end. Tape this piece in place and then repeat, working inwards in 1cm/²⁄₅in steps until you have a total of six semi-circles, as shown.

8 Wrap a 60cm/24in length of 0.5mm/¹⁄₅₀in wire once around the centre back struts. Hook the smallest semi-circle of wire into position on the back edge and firmly close the hooks.

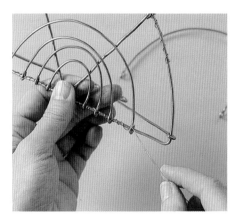

9 Wrap the fine wire around it to hold it in place, then repeat to attach the other semi-circles. Fasten off the fine wire tightly at the corners. Using the fine wire, attach the semi-circles to the shelf supports in the same way, first working in along one support and then working back out along the other.

10 Cut a 1.2m/47in length of 1.5mm/¹⁄₁₉in wire, and wrap it around a length of 1cm/²⁄₅in dowel to make a flattened coil. Pull out the coil so that it stretches evenly around the curved outside edge of the shelf, and bind it in place with a 60cm/24in length of 0.5mm/¹⁄₅₀in wire. Hang the shelf using a picture hook in each corner.

The elegance of this fresh green rack will add style to your kitchen and ensure that your kitchen implements, such as brushes and spoons, are always close at hand.

Spoon Rack

you will need
thick gardening wire
ruler or tape measure
wire cutters
rolling pin
round-nosed (snug-nosed) pliers
piece of copper piping
permanent marker pen
screwdriver and 4 screws

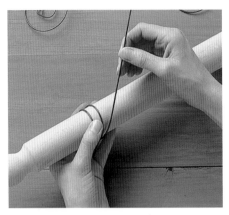

1 Cut three 1m/40in lengths of thick gardening wire. Wrap one end of each wire three times around a rolling pin. Using the round-nosed (snug-nosed) pliers, make a small loop in the coiled end of each wire large enough to take a screw. Shape the coils into a spiral in each wire. Bend back the wire from one of the lengths at a right angle to make the central stem.

2 To make the spoon holders, cut three 58cm/23in lengths of wire. Bend each wire at a right angle 12.5cm/5in from one end. In the next section of wire, make a row of three circles by wrapping the wire one and a half times around a piece of copper piping (or similar tube) for each of the circles.

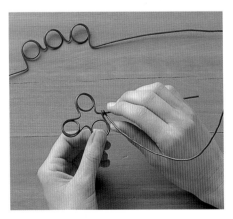

3 Bend the remaining wire away from the third circle at a right angle. Bend the three circles around to form a clover shape and bind the long end of wire around the 12.5cm/5in end for 7cm/2¾in. Do not cut off the ends.

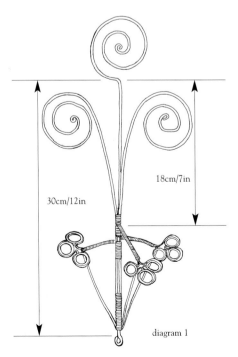

30cm/12in

18cm/7in

diagram 1

◀ **4** Arrange the three spiralled wires together with the right-angled one in the centre. Measure 30cm/12in down from the right angle on the central stem and then mark this point. Cut a 36cm/14in length of wire and make a small loop in one end. Leave 2cm/⅘in next to the loop, then bind the wire tightly around the spiralled wires, upwards from the marked point (see diagram 1).

5 Measure 18cm/7in from the right angle of the central stem (see diagram 1), and, using the excess wire on one of the clover shapes, bind it on to the stem at this point. Bind upwards for 2cm/⁴⁄₅in and cut off the wire. Bind on the second clover shape 2cm/⁴⁄₅in below the first in the same way. Attach the third shape below the second, binding downwards for 4cm/1½in. Make a bend halfway along the stems of the second and third clover shapes to angle them inwards slightly.

6 Bend up the three stem wires at the bottom and bind each to the neck of one of the clover shapes. Cut off the ends. Screw the spoon holder on to the wall through the loop in each spiral and at the bottom of the stem.

Grace your breakfast table with this sculptural toast rack. The tight wire wrapping and the star patterns on the handle and feet beads give the piece an original space-age quality.

Toast Rack

you will need

copper wire, 2.5mm/$\frac{1}{10}$in and 1mm/$\frac{1}{25}$in thick

ruler or tape measure

wire cutters

round-nosed (snug-nosed) pliers

tacking wire

bottle

file (optional)

permanent marker pen

strong glue

silver-plated copper wire, 0.8mm/$\frac{1}{31}$in thick

4 medium-sized beads

large star bead

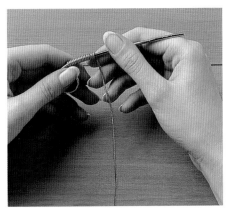

1 Cut a 10cm/4in length of 2.5mm/$\frac{1}{10}$in copper wire, and use round-nosed (snug-nosed) pliers to bend a loop in one end to make a "key". Attach the 1mm/$\frac{1}{25}$in copper wire next to the loop and wrap for 2cm/$\frac{4}{5}$in. Do not cut off the wire.

2 Cut two 25cm/10in lengths of 2.5mm/$\frac{1}{10}$in copper wire for the main shafts. Place the key at a right angle to one of the 25cm/10in lengths of wire, 1cm/$\frac{1}{2}$in from the end. Wrap the shaft with the same length of 1mm/$\frac{1}{25}$in wire for 23cm/9in by turning the key.

3 Remove the key from the initial 2cm/$\frac{4}{5}$in of wrapping and place at a right angle to the other end of the 25cm/10in piece of wire. Wrap the key for another 2cm/$\frac{4}{5}$in, making sure that this coil sticks out from the shaft wire on the same side as the first. Cut off the wrapping wire and remove the key from the coil.

4 Trim the shaft wire close to the coil at each end. Wrap the second shaft wire in exactly the same way. Cut two 35cm/13$\frac{3}{4}$in lengths of 2.5mm/$\frac{1}{10}$in wire. Wrap these wires in the same way again, leaving 7cm/2$\frac{3}{4}$in unwrapped at each end. Do not trim the unwrapped sections – these will form the legs.

5 Using pliers, adjust all the 2cm/$\frac{4}{5}$in coils so that they stick out from the wrapped wires at right angles and point in the same direction. To make the handles, cut two 21cm/8$\frac{1}{4}$in lengths of 2.5mm/$\frac{1}{10}$in wire. Make a 2cm/$\frac{4}{5}$in coil as before, then begin wrapping one of the wires 1cm/$\frac{1}{2}$in from the end. Wrap for 14cm/5$\frac{1}{2}$in.

▶

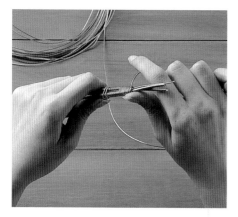

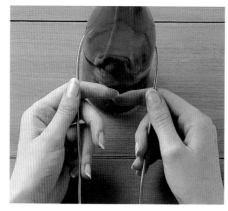

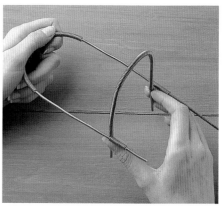

6 Trim the wrapping wire, leaving a long end. Wrap the second handle strut, but do not cut off the wrapping wire. Tack the two handle struts together using tacking wire, checking that the coils are facing in the same direction. Wrap them together, continuing up from the 14cm/5½in wrapped sections. Leave 2cm/⅘in at the top unwrapped.

7 To make the base, cut a 50cm/20in length of 2.5mm/¹⁄₁₀in wire. Leave 15cm/6in at one end and bend the next section around a bottle 6cm/2½in in diameter. Wrap another length of 2.5mm/¹⁄₁₀in wire for 12.5cm/5in. Trim the wrapping wire. Remove the length of wire and thread the 12.5cm/5in coil on to the bent wire. Move it along until it sits in the bend.

8 Bend each of the four wrapped pieces to make a curve in the centre. Thread the first wrapped section on the base. It should be one of the pieces with 7cm/2¾in legs. If you find it hard to push the wires through the coils, file the ends of the base wire. Pull apart the individually wrapped struts of the handle section and bend them to make an arch shape.

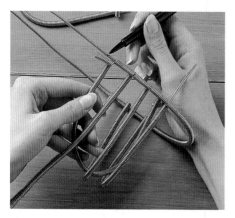

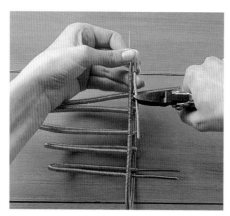

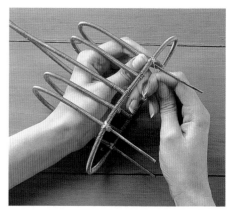

9 Thread on the next piece (with no legs), followed by the handle arch. Before threading on the next piece, mark the base wire halfway along the length of the next coil. You will cut the wire at this point later. Thread on this piece, followed by the second piece with legs. Wrap a length of 2.5mm/¹⁄₁₀in wire for 9cm/3½in and then remove the coil. Thread the 9cm/3½in coil on to the long end of the base wire.

10 Bend the wire to mirror the first curve and until the two wrapped sections meet. Cut off the wire where it meets the marked point. Remove the last two coils from the base wire and cut off at the marked point. Thread the first coil on to the base wire next to the curve. Slot half of the next coil back on to the other end of the base wire. Apply glue to the end of the base wire next to the curve and slot it into the empty section of the next coil. Allow to dry.

11 Using silver-plated copper wire, bind crosses around the leg joints to add stability. If you find that the rack is too springy, carefully apply a little glue to the joints. Make four 5cm/2in coils of 1mm/¹⁄₂₅in wire by wrapping around a length of 2.5mm/¹⁄₁₀in wire and then removing. Thread these coils on to the legs and then glue on bead feet. Glue the large bead on to the top of the handle. If necessary, make the hole in the bead a little larger by drilling carefully.

You don't need DIY skills to create fashionable designer furniture. Wooden chairs with a removable seat are easy to find. Paint the chair in one colour and choose wire of a contrasting colour.

Woven Chair

you will need

wooden chair

8 screw eyes

parallel (channel-type) pliers

enamelled copper wire in two colours, 2.5mm/¹⁄₁₀in and 1mm/¹⁄₂₅in thick

wire cutters

round-nosed (snug-nosed) pliers

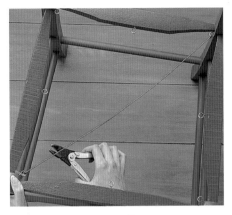

1 Screw the screw eyes into the inside of the chair frame, one in each corner of the seat section and one in the middle of each side piece, as shown. Tighten them securely with parallel (channel-type) pliers and make sure that all of the ring ends lie flat.

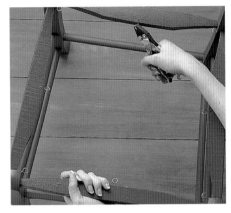

2 Attach the 2.5mm/¹⁄₁₀in wire to one corner by threading it through the eye and twisting the end around the wire, using pliers. Stretch it diagonally across the frame and secure it to the opposite eye. Repeat across the other diagonal. Make a diamond between the four side screws with four more pieces of wire.

3 Cut a long length of 1mm/¹⁄₂₅in enamelled copper wire and fold it in half. Attach it by passing the loop under the centre of the copper wire cross and threading the end back through to secure.

4 Weave a square so that you cover half the distance from the centre to the point where the copper wires cross. Cut off the wire, then wrap it around several times and tuck in the end. Weave four more squares, one at each point where the wires cross.

5 Attach another double length of 1mm/¹⁄₂₅in enamelled copper wire to one of the corner screw eyes.

▶

6 Weave first around one side of the chair frame, then work back around the diagonal copper wire and continue around the other side of the chair frame to make a herringbone pattern at the corner.

7 Continue weaving until you reach the square nearest to that corner. Secure the wire and trim, tucking in the end as before. Weave the other three corners of the chair in the same way.

8 Loop a double length of 1mm/$\frac{1}{25}$in enamelled copper wire around one of the side screw eyes. Weave around the chair frame to one side of the eye, then over the eye, around the other side of the chair frame and back under the eye. Continue in this way until the eye is completely covered.

9 Continue weaving by wrapping the wire around the two diagonal copper wires as well as the chair frame. Weave until you reach the two nearest squares. Secure the wire and cut it off. Weave the other three sides.

10 Stretch two lengths of 2.5mm/$\frac{1}{10}$in copper wire across each of the spaces between the five central woven squares. Attach the wire ends to the corners of the squares and secure with round-nosed (snug-nosed) pliers.

11 Use 1mm/$\frac{1}{25}$in enamelled copper wire in a second colour to weave a square in each space. Weave the four squares so that they are smaller than the first five and there are gaps in the finished pattern.

Copper wire is naturally warm in colour, and the wrapping technique used here enhances its rich appearance. The bowl looks particularly soft and sumptuous when displayed by candlelight.

Copper Bowl

you will need

copper wire, 2mm/¹⁄₁₃in, 0.8mm/¹⁄₃₁in, 2.5mm/¹⁄₁₀in, 1mm/¹⁄₂₅in and 1.5mm/¹⁄₁₉in thick

ruler or tape measure

wire cutters

parallel (channel-type) pliers

bowls in two sizes

quick-drying glue

permanent marker pen

general-purpose pliers

1 Cut eight 42cm/16½in lengths of 2mm/¹⁄₁₃in copper wire. Wrap with 0.8mm/¹⁄₃₁in wire. Make a coil with a diameter of about 4cm/1½in at one end and one of 2.5cm/1in at the other, using parallel (channel-type) pliers.

2 Bend each wire to form the curved side struts of the bowl. To make the rims of the bowl, cut two lengths of 2.5mm/¹⁄₁₀in wire, one 80cm/32in and the other 50cm/20in. Wrap the longer length in 1mm/¹⁄₂₅in wire and the shorter in 1.5mm/¹⁄₁₉in wire.

3 Release 2cm/⅘in at each end of the coil. Bend the longer wrapped wire around the larger bowl and the shorter wrapped wire around the smaller bowl to make two wire hoops.

4 Insert a little quick-drying glue into the empty end of each coil and slot in the projecting end of wire. Hold it firmly in place until the glue is dry.

5 Lightly mark eight equidistant points around each of the hoops. Cut 16 lengths of 1mm/¹⁄₂₅in wire, each measuring 12.5cm/5in. Use these to begin binding the side struts to the hoops. Allow the struts to extend above the top rim by 6cm/2½in and below the bottom rim by 4cm/1½in.

6 Continue to bind the struts to the hoops, wiring alternate ones first. This gives the bowl stability. Bind the last four struts to the hoops, adjusting any that become misshapen in the process.

7 Make an open coil with a diameter of 15cm/6in, from the 2.5mm/¹⁄₁₀in copper wire. Hold the shape of the spiral by binding it with two lengths of 1mm/¹⁄₂₅in copper wire, leaving about 10cm/4in spare wire at each end.

8 To attach the base coil, bind the excess wire around four of the struts. Twist a 2.3m/2½yd double length of 1mm/¹⁄₂₅in wire and wrap it around the bowl. Make a zigzag between the struts and halfway between the top struts.

Chicken wire becomes an exotic material when used to make this lantern, which is perfect for hanging in the garden. Place long-lasting night-lights in the jam jars.

Garden Lantern

you will need

gloves

small-gauge chicken wire

wire cutters

ruler or tape measure

aluminium wire, 1mm/$\frac{1}{25}$in thick

galvanized wire, 1.5mm/$\frac{1}{19}$in thick

round-nosed (snug-nosed) pliers

general-purpose pliers

bottle with cone-shaped lid

jam jar

large beads

bath-plug chain

metal ring

flat-headed jewellery pins

narrow ribbon (optional)

1 Wearing gloves, cut one piece of chicken wire 18 × 61cm/7 × 24in and one piece 22 × 55cm/8½ x 21½in. Form two cylinders with the wire and join the short edges together with the aluminium wire. Cut one length of the galvanized wire 66cm/26in and one length 61cm/24in. Bend to form two hoops with the same diameter. Bind the ends with aluminium wire.

2 Use the aluminium wire to bind a hoop on to the edge of each cylinder. To shape the large cylinder into the lantern, carefully bend each of the holes in the chicken wire into heart shapes (see Basic Techniques). Use round-nosed (snug-nosed) pliers and your hands to mould the cylinder. (If necessary, refer to the step 7 picture for guidance with the shape.)

3 To make the lid, bend all the holes in the second cylinder into heart shapes, then mould the wire to form a curved lid shape. You will need to squash the holes together at the top.

4 Using the hollow section in the mouth of the general-purpose pliers, carefully crimp the chicken wire in the centre of each section to give you a central core.

5 Form a long cone for the lid. Wrap the aluminium wire around the tapered top of a paint or glue bottle. The bottom of the cone must fit over the central core of the lid.

6 Secure a length of thin wire inside the centre of the lid and push it through the core. Thread the coiled cone on to the wire and slip over the core. Leave the length of wire hanging loose from the centre of the cone. Wrap another length of wire around the core of the lantern section to make a smaller coil.

7 Cut four 10cm/4in pieces of the galvanized wire. Using round-nosed pliers, bend each piece into a loop with a hook at each end. Curve up the bend in each loop slightly. Position evenly around the rim of the lantern section and close up the hooks with pliers. Cut two lengths of galvanized wire and twist together around the neck of a jam jar so that the ends stick out on each side. Attach the wires to the lantern rim on each side of two opposite loops. This will hold the jam jar securely in place.

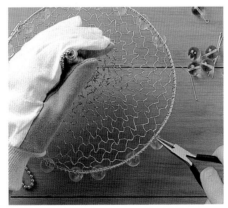

8 Thread a large metallic bead on to the loose wire in the lid. Bind the bath-plug chain on to the wire and trim any excess. Attach a metal ring to the other end for hanging. Thread beads on to flat-headed jewellery pins and hang evenly around the rim. Add a large bead to the lantern core.

9 Put the lid on the lantern and slot the four loops on the lantern rim through the chicken wire of the lid. Press them down firmly. It is very important for safety that the loops hold the bottom securely in place. Reinforce with extra pieces of wire or tie with narrow ribbon.

Instead of balancing them precariously on a tray, a bottle and glasses can be safely carried into the garden in this stylish and sturdy carrier made from wire and bamboo.

Garden Drinks Carrier

you will need

black bamboo canes

ruler or tape measure

saw

skewer or length of thick wire

broom handle

galvanized wire, 2mm/$\frac{1}{13}$in and 1mm/$\frac{1}{25}$in thick

wire cutters

flat-nosed pliers

food can

fine wire

plastic coated garden wire, or length of thick wire 3.5mm/$\frac{1}{7}$in thick

length of plastic tubing (aquarium air line)

1 From the black bamboo canes, cut eight 15cm/6in lengths for the base of the drinks carrier and eight 17cm/6¾in lengths for the uprights. Use a skewer or length of thick wire to remove the pith from the centre of each cane.

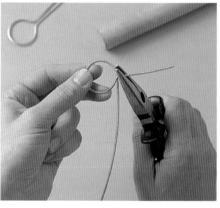

2 To make each glass carrier, use the broom handle to turn a loop in the end of a length of the 2mm/$\frac{1}{13}$in galvanized wire. Bend the short end to lie against the length and then thread both ends of the wire through the centre of one of the hollowed-out base canes.

3 Measure 8cm/3¼in along the wire from the end of the cane, and at this point form a circle around a can. Twist the end around the wire to secure, and cut off the excess. Repeat to make eight base cane sections.

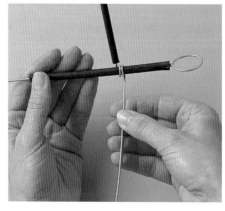

4 Make eight more looped wire lengths and thread them through the upright canes. Use the end of the wire to bind each upright cane to a base cane, 8cm/3¼in from the end with the small loop, and trim.

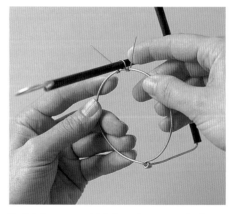

5 Make two 90° bends in each long wire, one at the end of the base cane and the other before the ring, and bind the ring to the upright with a short length of fine wire.

6 When the eight sections are all completed, arrange them in a circle, laying down each pair of opposites together. Using fine wire, bind all the central loops together and bind the rings to each other.

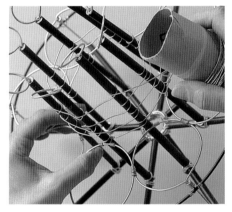

7 Cut a length of the plastic-coated garden wire to fit around the edge of the carrier and twist the ends to make a circle. Use fine wire to bind this in place just under each ring, and to bind the upright canes together. Turn the carrier upside down and loop fine wire around the base canes to make a firm platform for the glasses.

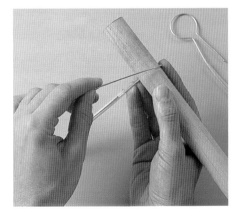

8 To make the carrying handles, use the broom handle to form a loop in one end of two short and two long lengths of wire and thread the wire into two lengths of plastic tubing (aquarium air line). Form another loop at the other end of the wires.

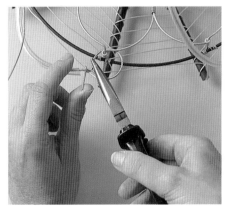

9 Thread the loops of the two long carrying handles through the loops at the top of four uprights, and secure them by twisting the ends of the wires around the handles. Attach the short handles around the garden wire ring in the same way.

Keep your herb and spice jars neat in this heart-rimmed rack, which is designed to hold five standard-sized spice jars. It can be hung on the wall or used free-standing on a shelf or kitchen surface.

Spice Rack

you will need

galvanized wire, 1.5mm/$\frac{1}{19}$in and 0.8mm/$\frac{1}{31}$in thick

ruler or tape measure

wire cutters

permanent marker pen

round-nosed (snug-nosed) pliers

general-purpose pliers

galvanized wire, 1.5mm/$\frac{1}{19}$in thick, doubled and twisted

tacking wire

broom handle

1 Cut five 45cm/18in lengths of the 1.5mm/$\frac{1}{19}$in wire. Mark at intervals of 5cm/2in, 5cm/2in, 25cm/10in, 5cm/2in and 5cm/2in.

2 Using round-nosed (snug-nosed) pliers, bend the 5cm/2in sections at the ends of each wire into coils. Using general-purpose pliers, bend each at right angles at the next 5cm/2in marks. Cut two 45cm/18in lengths of twisted wire and mark in the same way. Untwist 5cm/2in at each end and make two coils. Bend right angles at the next marks.

3 Cut two 9cm/3½in lengths of 1.5mm/$\frac{1}{19}$in galvanized wire. Make the box section of the spice rack by joining together the two twisted wire struts. Twist the ends of the 9cm/3½in lengths around the bent corners of the struts, leaving a distance of 6cm/2½in between the two struts.

4 Cut a 104cm/41in length of twisted wire and mark it at intervals of 20cm/8in, 12.5cm/5in, 6cm/2½in, 25cm/10in, 6cm/2½in, 12.5cm/5in and 20cm/8in. Bend at the marked points to form a rectangle and heart.

5 Attach the four corners of the heart rim to the top of the box section using tacking wire. Cut four 54.5cm/21½in lengths of twisted wire and mark each at intervals of 5cm/2in, 5cm/2in, 6cm/2½in and 38cm/15in.

6 Untwist the 5cm/2in end of each wire and make into two coils. Bend right angles at the next two marked points. Bend each 38cm/15in section into a coil. Bend a curve in the wire next to two of the coils.

7 Slot the box section inside these four pieces so that the four large coils are at the back beside the heart. Tack into place where the pieces touch.

8 Slot the plain wire struts made in step 1 inside the box structure. Space them evenly across the width of the box and tack into place.

9 Wrap a long length of 1.5mm/¹⁄₁₉in galvanized wire several times around a broom handle to make a loose coil. Flatten the coil and position it inside the front edge of the spice rack.

10 Using 0.8mm/¹⁄₃₁in galvanized wire, bind around the top rim of the box, securing each piece in position and removing the tacking wire as you go. Then bind from front to back along the bottom struts. Finish the spice rack by binding the heart closed at the top and bottom. Bind all of the decorative spirals where they touch.

One of the great things about wire is that it gives structure to otherwise flimsy materials. Here the wire used is completely covered with raffia to create a rustic tray.

Garden Tray

1 For the handles, cut two 1m/40in lengths of wire. Using a marker pen, mark each wire at intervals of 25cm/10in, 5cm/2in, 40cm/16in, 5cm/2in and 25cm/10in.

2 Using parallel (channel-type) pliers, bend each wire at the marked points into two handle shapes. The 25cm/10in sections double up to form the tray base. The two 5cm/2in sections make the sides and the long 40cm/16in section curves over the top. Hold each handle together at the base with double-sided adhesive tape.

3 To make the hearts, cut two 1m/40in lengths of straining wire and mark at intervals of 38cm/15in, 25cm/10in, and 38cm/15in. Make the middle section into a heart shape and cross the wires over at the marked points. Bend up the wire and then secure it with tape. Wrap the heart wires and the handles with tape, then bind them closely with raffia.

4 Using round-nosed (snug-nosed) pliers, bend the ends of the heart wires into coils, so that they will fit inside the handles.

5 Place the mat inside the handle. Bind in place with raffia. Thread the raffia between the mat sticks and also around the sides and base of the handle. Place the heart inside the handle. Bind in place.

6 Bind the second handle and heart wire to the other end of the mat. Make two bundles of twigs and bind tightly to the top of the handles with double-sided adhesive tape. Wrap with raffia to cover all the tape.

A rack of hooks is always useful, and can be hung in the hall for keys, in the bathroom for towels and in the kitchen for utensils. This project is ideal to make with children, as the plastic-coated wire is safe to use.

Kitchen Hook Rack

you will need

green gardening wire

broom handle

ruler or tape measure

wire cutters

permanent marker pen

pencil

wooden spoon

screwdriver and 3 screws

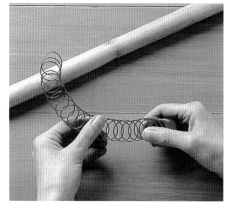

1 Tightly wrap the gardening wire 40 times around a broom handle. Leave 10cm/4in of wire at each end and cut off. Flatten the coil. The coil should be about 30cm/12in long.

2 Cut a 56cm/22in length of wire. Mark the centre and the point 15cm/6in from each end. Form a loop at each of the points by wrapping the wire around a pencil. Thread the wire through the flattened coil, and then thread the circle at each end of the coil through the end loops on the wire.

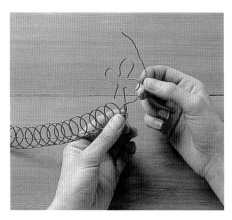

3 Bend the 15cm/6in section at each end of the gardening wire around the handle of a wooden spoon to create a three-leaf clover shape, as shown. There should be about 2cm/¾in left at the end to bend back down the stem. Use the 10cm/4in of wire left at the ends of the coil to bind the stem.

4 Cut four 30cm/12in lengths of wire. Bend each in half and wrap the bend around the handle of a wooden spoon to make a circle. Twist to close. Bend small hooks in the ends of the wires. Bend each wire in half. Loop the hooks around the coil and bottom wire of the frame, and close tightly.

5 Cut a 2m/79in length of wire. Bend in half, wrap the bend around the handle of a wooden spoon to make a circle. Twist closed. Mark 15cm/6in from the circle. Ask a friend to hold this point while you twist the wires, then bend them around the broom to make a clover shape. Bind closed.

◀ **6** To finish, slot the clover hook through the middle of the coil, so that its shank lies on either side of the central loop in the base wire. Bend up the hook 5cm/2in from the circle end. Screw the rack to the wall through the three loops in the bottom wire. The central screw holds the hook firmly in place.

The shelf at the bottom of this simply designed rack is wide enough to hold four food cans. Stripped of their labels, the cans make useful storage containers that complement the design of the rack.

Utility Rack

you will need

straining wire

ruler or tape measure

wire cutters

permanent marker pen

round-nosed (snug-nosed) pliers

galvanized wire, 0.8mm/$\frac{1}{31}$in and 1.5mm/$\frac{1}{19}$in thick

general-purpose pliers

tacking wire

gloves

small-gauge chicken wire

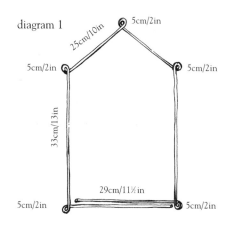

diagram 1

1 To make the frame, cut a 2m/79in length of straining wire. Twist the ends to stop them from unravelling. Mark the wire at intervals of 29cm/11½in, 5cm/2in, 33cm/13in, 5cm/2in, 25cm/10in, 5cm/2in, 25cm/10in, 5cm/2in, 33cm/13in, 5cm/2in, and 29cm/11½in.

2 Using round-nosed (snug-nosed) pliers, make a loop with each 5cm/2in section, making sure that the pen marks match up and that all the loops face outwards (see diagram 1). Using the 0.8mm/$\frac{1}{31}$in wire, bind the 29cm/11½in sections together to make the bottom of the frame.

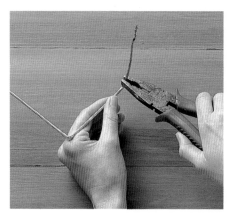

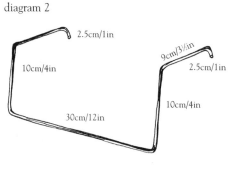

diagram 2

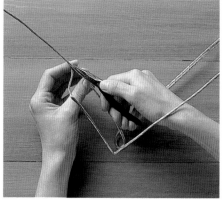

3 To make the shelf, cut a 73.5cm/29in length of straining wire and mark it at intervals of 2.5cm/1in, 9cm/3½in, 10cm/4in, 30cm/12in, 10cm/4in, 9cm/3½in and 2.5cm/1in. Using general-purpose pliers, bend the wire at right angles at the marked points (see diagram 2).

4 Mark each side of the frame 10cm/4in from the bottom. Twist the 2.5cm/1in ends of the shelf wire tightly around the frame at these points.

5 For the rim and sides of the shelf, cut a 104cm/41in length of 1.5mm/ ¹⁄₁₉in galvanized wire and mark it at intervals of 2.5cm/1in, 12.5cm/5in, 9cm/3½in, 12.5cm/5in, 30cm/12in, 12.5cm/5in, 9cm/3½in, 12.5cm/5in and 2.5cm/1in. Using round-nosed pliers, make a loop with the 2.5cm/1in section at each end of the wire. Bend the wire at the 12.5cm/5in and 9cm/3½in points at each end at 45° angles to form the side crosses of the shelf. Bend the 30cm/12in section in the middle at right angles to form the top rim (see diagram 3).

diagram 3

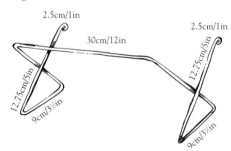

6 Tack the loops at the ends of the rim wire to the 10cm/4in markings on the sides of the main frame. Tack each corner of the side crosses to the frame.

◀ **7** Lay the frame on to a piece of chicken wire and cut around the frame. Allow 30cm/12in at the bottom for wrapping around the shelf, so that there is a double thickness of wire at the front of the shelf where it tucks inside. Using 0.8mm/¹⁄₃₁in galvanized wire, bind the edges of the chicken wire to the frame. Wrap any rough edges at the top around the frame before binding. Bind the shelf firmly to the frame as you bind on the chicken wire, and remove the tacking wire.

Small aluminium drink (soda) cans and aluminium mesh form the basis of this bird feeder. It can be filled with various types of nuts, scraps and larger seeds.

Wire Bird Feeder

you will need

small aluminium drink (soda) cans

old scissors

permanent marker pen

aluminium mesh

wire cutters

small pliers

bradawl (awl)

galvanized wire

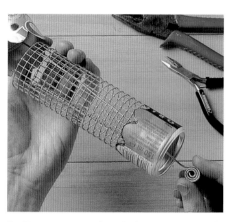

1 Cut a small aluminium drink (soda) can in half, then draw a decorative scalloped border around each half with a permanent marker pen and cut out. Trim off any jagged edges with a pair of old scissors.

2 Cut a rectangle of aluminium mesh to fit, rolled up, inside the can. Join the edges by hooking the cut ends through the mesh and bending them over, using pliers. Pierce a hole in the bottom of the can. Fit the mesh cylinder into the two halves of the can, then thread on to galvanized wire. Coil the lower end of the wire so that the feeder cannot slide off.

3 Leave a length of wire above the top of the can long enough for the top to slide up off the mesh, for refilling, then add 7.5cm/3in. Cut the wire. Twist the end into a flat coil, make a hook by bending the wire over a pen. Repeat.

Templates

Enlarge the templates on a photocopier. Alternatively, trace the design and draw a grid of evenly spaced squares over your tracing. Draw a larger grid on to another piece of paper and copy the outline square by square. Finally, draw over the lines to make sure they are continuous.

Window Box Edging, p24–25

Panelled Flower Pot Cover, p22–23

Greetings Cards, p28

Greetings Cards, p28

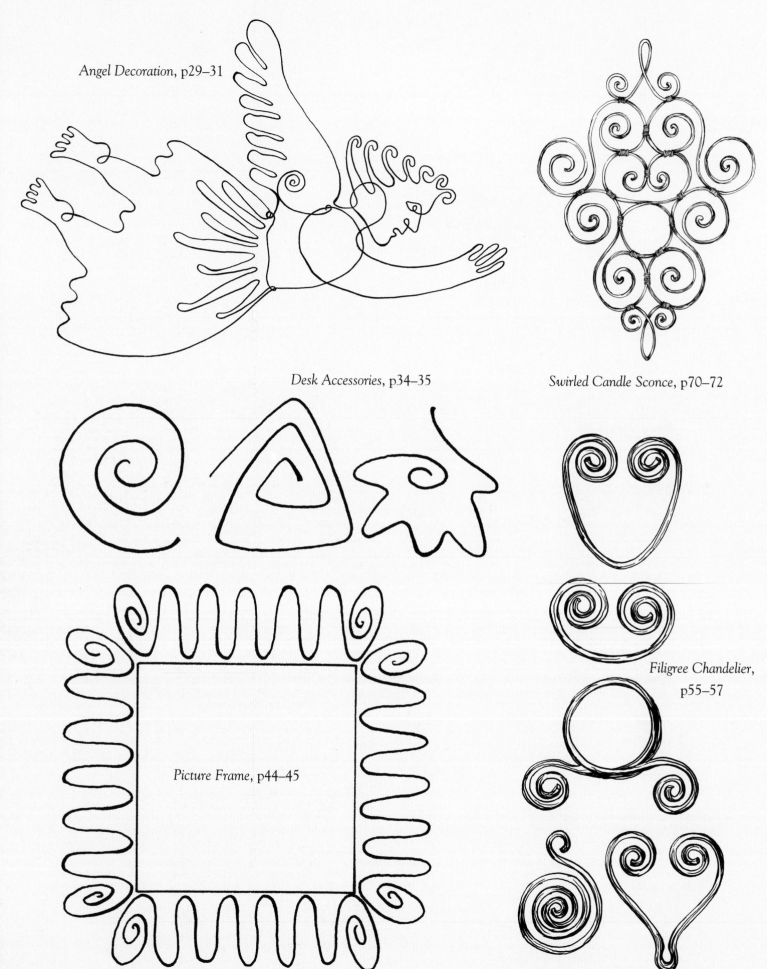

Angel Decoration, p29–31

Swirled Candle Sconce, p70–72

Desk Accessories, p34–35

Filigree Chandelier,
p55–57

Picture Frame, p44–45

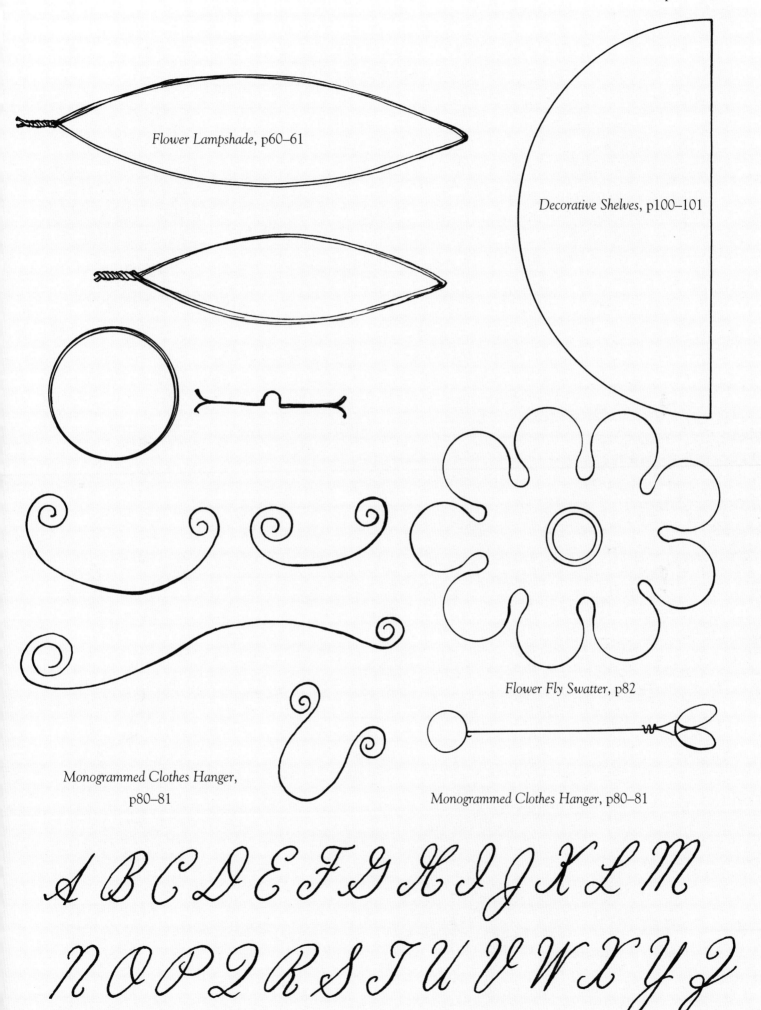

Flower Lampshade, p60–61

Decorative Shelves, p100–101

Flower Fly Swatter, p82

Monogrammed Clothes Hanger,
p80–81

Monogrammed Clothes Hanger, p80–81

A B C D E F G H I J K L M

N O P Q R S T U V W X Y Z

Index